The
Anabaptists
Are
Back

Blessed are the peacemakers,
for they will be called
children of God.

The Anabaptists Are Back

MAKING PEACE IN A DANGEROUS WORLD

Duane Ruth-Heffelbower
Stories collected by Phillip Stoltzfus
Foreword by Gene Stoltzfus

HERALD PRESS
Scottdale, Pennsylvania
Waterloo, Ontario

Library of Congress Cataloging-in-Publication Data
Ruth-Heffelbower, Duane, 1949-
    The Anabaptists are back : making peace in a dangerous world /
Duane Ruth Heffelbower.
        p.   cm.
    Includes bibliographical references.
    ISBN 0-8361-3552-0 (alk. paper)
        1. Peace—Religious aspects—Christianity. 2. Nonviolence—
Religious aspects—Christianity. 3. Historic peace churches.
4. Anabaptists. 5. Government, Resistance to—Religious aspects—
Christianity. I. Title.
BT736.4.R89   1991
261.8'73—dc20   91-6668
                                                                        CIP

The paper used in this publication is recycled and meets the minimum
requirements of American National Standard for Information
Sciences—Permanence of Paper for Printed Library Materials, ANSI
Z39.48-1984.

THE ANABAPTISTS ARE BACK
Copyright © 1991 by Herald Press, Scottdale, Pa. 15683
    Published simultaneously in Canada by Herald Press,
    Waterloo, Ont. N2L 6H7. All rights reserved.
Library of Congress Catalog Number: 91-6668
International Standard Book Number: 0-8361-3552-0
Printed in the United States of America
Book and cover design by Gwen Stamm

1 2 3 4 5 6 7 8 9 10 97 96 95 94 93 92 91

Contents

Foreword

As this important book went to print, the war in the Persian Gulf was stirring global anxiety. People of faith looked for the glory of God beyond the misplaced cross of war. The faithful saw God's mighty acts reaching inside that line in the desert into the hearts of love and tenderness God has placed in all peoples.

The Anabaptists Are Back is a compelling introduction to activist peacemaking. It interweaves and gives energy for decision making, jail life, spiritual preparation, and faith for the work.

The book's stories and its rationale for peacemaking arise from a decade when North America was misusing power in Central America. That period's experiences in peacemaking prepared us for the gulf crisis (and that crisis prepared us for future ones).

Prior to war, people prayed, were arrested, and cried out against war. A Christian Peacemaker Team went to Iraq, seeking a table where Iraqi-United States talks could take place. We may doubt our success, but someday, when the secret files of the period become public, we may be astonished at the effects of our spirit-based actions.

The stories in this book show that every generation can rediscover the wonderful possibilities of God's reign amidst world events. Members of peace churches celebrate the long struggle for conscientious objection, a right the world's nations are just now granting. People prayed, lobbied, even died to achieve this. We can act today because former generations prepared the way.

No longer isolated from the world, our churches are deeply involved. This book lays a framework for positive, prophetic, and critical engagement in our day. The "new world order" the world's powerful nations envision will require massive military commitments. The mighty will seek to control world resources for those at the top of the world pyramid. The gulf crisis is one of many times when people of faith and justice will need to publicly unmask this order's deception and sin.

As we become peacemakers, we must root our work in and evaluate it from a practical and biblical perspective. This book teaches us to do peacemaking with the Bible in one hand and the newspaper in the other.

Authentic action is not only a response to guilt. It flows from a dream that someday the sons and daughters of communists and Christians will frolic together; Arab as well as North American children will enjoy the earth's fruits; the tanks will be melted into playground equipment; the full glory of God will be revealed and all flesh, united will see it.

—*Gene Stoltzfus*
Christian Peacemaker Teams/Synapses
Chicago, Illinois

Author's Preface

"Blessed are the peacemakers," said Jesus. He didn't say "peace lovers." Christians have not always seen the difference.

This book looks at how the spiritual descendants of the sixteenth-century Anabaptists are rediscovering peace-*making* and asks what it may mean to be peacemakers in a dangerous world.

In 1984, Ron Sider called for teams of Christian peace-makers who would step between warring parties. Since then, interest in this active, potentially dangerous, peace-making has grown. Why, Sider asked, do soldiers battle while peacemakers stay home? Shouldn't peacemakers be where the battle is? Shouldn't they be as willing to die for peace as soldiers are to die in war?

Christian Peacemaker Teams is an organization created by several historic peace churches (Mennonite Church, General Conference Mennonite Church, Church of the Brethren, and the Brethren in Christ). It aims to put peace-makers in harm's way—to send peacemakers into places of conflict as advocates for a peaceful and just resolution.

Christian Peacemaker Teams were involved in peacemaking between the Canadian government and the Mohawk Nation in Quebec. Violence still broke out. CPT also sent representatives to Iraq to advocate a peaceful solution to the crisis created by Iraq's invasion of Kuwait. They were warmly received, but no negotiations took place. War began January 16, 1991.

Active peacemaking enters the heart of conflict. It can look more like troublemaking than peacemaking. That is the risk people take when they live out Jesus' call. This book includes stories of people trying to live out Jesus' call in ways you may not like. Suspend judgment for a while. Read these stories as the sincere efforts of brothers and sisters in Christ to take Jesus and the ministry of reconciliation seriously.

"For in Christ all the fullness of God was pleased to dwell, and through Christ to reconcile to God all things, whether on earth or in heaven, making peace by the blood of his cross" (Col. 1:19-20).[1] Jesus said, "Blessed are the peacemakers, for they will be called children of God" (Matt. 5:9, NRSV).

The stories in this book, unless otherwise noted, were collected by Phillip Stoltzfus, the first Christian Peacemaker Teams volunteer. Phil traveled around North America interviewing people involved in active peacemaking. Thanks to him and to the people who told him their stories. They made this book possible.

Thanks are also due to my wife and copastor, Clare Ann; son, Andrew; and Peace Community Church—Mennonite of Clovis, California, who shared me with this book for a longer time than they expected.

—*Duane Ruth-Heffelbower*
Fresno, California

CHAPTER 1
A Bridge of Stories

Some Stories to Start With

It is one thing to think about peace. It is another thing to make peace in real life. This book tries to bridge the gap through true stories of people who tried to make peace, each in their own way, each with different results.

Sometimes the stories illustrate a point. Sometimes they simply raise new questions. All of the storytellers are honestly struggling to find God's will for their lives. Perhaps their experiences will help you as you try to live a life faithful to God.

Bill Kaye grew up in a military family and was drafted into the Vietnam War. After a lengthy readjustment period following the war and several years of graduate work, he began attending the Seattle Mennonite Church, Seattle, Washington. He also involved himself in social issues. At the time he told this story he was working with homeless persons at the Seattle Downtown Emergency Shelter.

In December 1987 Bill and pastoral intern Carol Rose

went to El Salvador to act as international observers accompanying refugees in conflicted zones. Two months after his return, Kaye spoke to his church about his experiences.

A lot of people in El Salvador have been fleeing to Honduras because their lives are threatened. In October 1987 about 4,300 of them from the Mesa Grande refugee camp in Honduras decided to go back all at once. They resettled about five villages in El Salvador. Our group visited Las Vueltas, one of these villages.

Las Vueltas is a town of about 1,000 people, six to seven hundred of them children. The town had been bombed by the army, and we saw the twenty-foot-deep crater made by a 500-pound bomb.

Almost everyone I talked to in Las Vueltas told me half their family had been murdered in extremely vicious ways. They would be raped in front of their families, then murdered. It was incredible to hear these stories. But these people decided to go back, even though the situation hadn't really changed. The Arias Peace Plan had provisions in it for refugees repopulating their home villages.

The villagers returned in October because that is the start of the dry season in El Salvador. They wanted to have all their buildings built before May, when the rains begin.

At the time we visited them, they had brought in a fresh water supply, built latrines, planted a two-acre garden, and built the basic structures for houses. We took money down to them which we had raised to buy siding for the houses.

December 24 is the day they do most of their Christmas celebrating. Part of the celebration is a one-event rodeo. The men ride horses down the main street, trying to grab, with a pin, a little ring hanging from a rope. They go racing past at full gallop. It looked very hard to me. I would have a terrible time just staying on the horse, but some of them did catch the ring.

During the rodeo there was a battle up in the hills. We heard M-16 and M-60 machine guns, and explosions which were probably hand grenades. The battle went on for several minutes. They told us later it was less than half a mile away.

Everything stopped during the battle. People stood there looking at each other. A few ran into the buildings. One woman cried.

But there was a sense, in spite of the battle, that they would go on. This kind of thing wasn't going to disrupt their lives. They knew what they were doing when they came back. They knew that this, and probably worse, would happen. But they had come back to stay in El Salvador, no matter what.

We internationals were helping. It's called *accompaniment*. By our presence, we made it unlikely that the army would do anything outrageous in the area. We learned that the fight in the hills was generally considered an accident. The guerrillas and the army had accidentally walked into each other. Because we internationals were present, there was little chance that anything would happen to the people of Las Vueltas, so the horse races went on.

On Christmas Day we went to the next town, up the road about three kilometers away, for mass. The villagers waited for the internationals so we could go to the village together. Coming back, they stayed with us, too. Every time we went anywhere, there were five or six Las Vueltans standing around. At the same time we were accompanying them, they were accompanying us.

Coming back from the service, we went through the hills on a path. I was first in line. I'm a Vietnam veteran and "pulled point" a few times in Vietnam, leading my squad through the jungle. This was like going back and pulling point again.

I looked back over my shoulder. People snaked behind me. They were too close together. As Vietnam taught, "one round will get you all." The idea in Vietnam was to spread out so that a hand grenade or something wouldn't kill everybody.

As I walked ahead, I found my eyes darting around, like

they used to in Vietnam, looking for flashes of metal that would be rifles. At the same time, I was eighteen years older, walking with a camera over my shoulder. I smiled at how ridiculous it was.

I'm sure the soldiers could see me, this touristy-looking American walking in front of a bunch of Salvadorans down the trail. I was protecting them as if they were GI's in Vietnam—only without a gun.

* * *

I live in Seattle and go to a Mennonite church. The church is fairly conscious of social issues, but it was amazing to be around people in El Salvador. Every one was so much more conscious about so many more things than I, because they were living it. Everything they did was for survival. They had to live together, they had to work on things. In North America we don't have to do that.

This is El Salvador. There is a new kind of person here. These are the most committed people I've met, more connected with their Christianity than most Americans. They remind one of many stories in the Bible. They are like the children of Israel returning to the Promised Land. When they see the struggles of Jesus, they see their own struggles.

I learned a lot about pacifism and the risks you have to take, and how much you can grow by taking risks. Jesus took a lot of risks. At the end of the road of risks is a better life—more social justice, more commitment, and a better feeling in yourself.

A former soldier "walking point" with a camera instead of a gun. Is this what we mean by "making peace in a dangerous world"? The next story comes closer to home for most of us. Instead of Central America, it takes place in the green hills of Concord, California. It could just as well be set in Pennsylvania, Iowa, or Texas.

Ruth Buxman, former pastor of First Mennonite Church

in San Francisco, describes an Easter sunrise service which pastor Phil Harrington and others organized at Concord (California) Naval Weapons Station in 1982.

It was a gorgeous day. The congregation went out early in the morning to the Concord Naval Weapons Station. Since it was spring, the hills were green. We went up a hill in a pastoral setting. You'd look around and expect to see cows grazing. But what we were looking down on looked like large graves covered with grass. That was where the weapons were buried in bunkers.

We sang and read Scripture. We prayed for nations and peoples affected by weapons from this particular place. The weapons stored here are sent to the third world, to Central America, to the Philippines. The last thing we did was release helium balloons, to represent rising and freedom.

The contrast between our celebration of Christ's rising from the grave and the graves holding destructive weapons was extremely vivid for me. We were celebrating life that day in a setting of death.

It is central to the celebration of Christianity to bring the promise of life right into the place of death. It made the connection strong for me. It opened my eyes. I didn't go out and do civil disobedience after that or become really involved in the peace community, but it opened my eyes to a lot of things. It opened my heart.

The Easter service was more about celebrating our faith than making a point to anybody. It wasn't planned to be a witness to anyone but those present. Easter became not just remembering the historical event of Jesus rising from the dead. It became a celebration that in this setting suddenly became a real thing involving real people.

To me, that is what the church has always said: the Jesus event affects our lives every day. It wasn't just a nice religious story to celebrate year after year as something that happened in the past, but a story whose reality and continuing meaning we can celebrate today. We see the evidence of death so often today, and that makes the resurrection story and its promise of life more necessary.

Making peace in a dangerous world can happen in many ways. Performing acts which save people and celebrating the act which saved all people are both part of it.

Violence, Nonviolence, and Nonresistance

Definitions are both important and difficult when we deal with peacemaking. One purpose of this book is to create a useful definition of peacemaking. The terms *violence* and *nonviolence* are common, and there is at least some agreement on what those words mean. *Nonresistance,* on the other hand, is a term used mostly by members of the historic peace churches to describe a particular type of nonviolence.

Rather than beginning with a dry definition, here is a true story, as told by Helen Quintela, about an experience she and her husband, Alberto, had. Included are three possible endings.

> When the group of our friends had gathered, Alberto began the painful recounting of our months of fear and intimidation. At many points he broke into tears. For the first time I fully realized what a terrible toll the months of our ordeal had taken on him.
>
> Alberto's recitation of the incidents created a vivid picture of the environment of abuse and violence in which we had been living, as our next-door neighbors tried to drive us from our home.
>
> Finally, Alberto explained our need for a seven-day continuing presence of friends in our home. In his words, "We have lost this home. We no longer feel safe here. Helen and I are asking you to help us regain our home, to help us feel at peace here again."

The first ending:

> That night thirty young men armed with clubs, chains, and guns surrounded the house of the people who had been harassing Alberto and Helen. A brick smashed the living room window, bringing a man bounding out onto the porch with a shotgun. Seeing he was outnumbered, he hesitated.
>
> "My friend," said one of the young men, "the next time Alberto tells us you have troubled him, we will level your house with you in it. Do you understand? If you do, lay your gun on the porch and go back inside."
>
> The man laid the gun on the porch and went inside. One of the young men picked up the shotgun. The group dissolved into the darkness.

This is the way of violence. It is the way many people live. To suggest any other way makes little sense to these people. Might does not make right, but it can make people leave you alone. People attracted to this way desire violent force to protect them from enemies. They ask for strong police or military protection in their city or country.

When you deal with dangerous people, you must meet them at their level. This understanding results in police officers being called "peace officers." Peace is something to be maintained by a threat of force which makes a violent attack too costly for the enemy. "You bother my friend; I level your house."

This used to be the only violence people recognized. Today we recognize violence in more subtle forms. We see that any action which takes away people's dignity harms them as surely as a punch in the nose. Now we see violence when people are treated badly because of their race, color, sex, age, or religious beliefs. Whenever a group of people wants to end discrimination against itself, one of its first tasks is to show others that the discrimination is a form of violence.

Drawing lines between "violent" and "not violent" has become ever more difficult. Where is the line, for instance, between child discipline and child abuse? Where is the line between setting job qualifications and improper discrimination?

Is it improper discrimination to have height and weight standards for airline flight attendants? The flight attendants think so. Is it violence when flight attendants lose their jobs because their airline wants thinner flight attendants? Is your answer different if the airline only wants white flight attendants?

At the level of international peacemaking, few would disagree that a landlord bulldozing the homes of striking banana plantation workers is violent. But is it violent for the International Monetary Fund to require higher loan payments from a poor country—resulting in children not receiving measles vaccine?

Recognizing that *violence* covers many kinds of action,[1] and that any book needs to fit between two covers, we will need to limit our discussion to a certain aspect of violence. For our purposes, violence will mean one of two related things: *(1) using* literal *physical force to harm people; or (2) using the* threat *of force to manipulate people against their will.*

While neither the flight attendants nor the IMF situations would fit this definition, most forms of child and sexual abuse would. We will continue to test this working definition as we move along.

The second ending to our story:

"Alberto," said one of his friends, "you are a lawyer; you know how to handle such people. Why don't you take care of yourself? It's not right for you to suffer and do nothing. Get a restraining order. Sue them for intentional infliction of emotional distress. They'll spend a lot of money defending themselves and will have to leave you alone. We can testify to the terrible things they have done."

"You're right," Alberto agreed. "Come back tomorrow night to sign the affidavits. We'll get that restraining order and have them in jail every time they violate it."

This is the nonviolent ending, right? Wrong. The threatened harm is more civilized. But it is just as physical as the first ending. Using police and courts is better than using goon squads, but the results are more similar than we like to think. When a police officer comes to your door to enforce a court order, which is what Alberto plans, the officer is ready to use physical force if necessary.

The real ending of the story:

> We prayed. Each of us lit a candle to symbolize the beginning of the peace vigil. People signed up for four-to-seven-hour shifts through the coming week. As they finished signing, they expressed their support and commitment to us.
>
> When everyone had left we turned to each other, a hint of joy in our faces. We were not alone anymore. We could already feel our church's and friends' presence of love and support.
>
> A lot of people asked, "Who were those people who came and stayed with you?" Nobody had heard of Mennonites. We did a series of seminars and radio programs addressed to the community on peace and justice issues. We tried to develop an awareness of alternatives to violence, and to explain who Mennonites were.
>
> My husband and I view our church as growing out of the racial situation that was present in the community. Our main objective is to be a presence in the community. We want to invite people into a "community of presence" that models a peaceful presence and helps establish a community of hope.

> I think our peace and justice issues are very family and community oriented. Family justice is interconnected with neighborhood justice and community justice.

This is the nonviolent ending, but it is also more than that. This ending demonstrates nonresistance. When nonresistant persons are attacked, they absorb the violence. They maintain avenues for reconciliation with the attacker, rather than offering violence in return. This is not a passive but a dynamic way of responding to violence.

Its goals are to turn enemies into friends through the power of love and to love enemies as we love ourselves, no matter what the result. Members of historic peace churches see nonresistance as the way of Jesus and the way for anyone who is Jesus' disciple. We will see other examples of this kind of nonviolence which seeks to make of the attacker a friend.

One mistake often made in describing the differences among violence, nonviolence, and nonresistance is to think that nonresistance and nonviolence are nonconfrontational.[2] Some nonresistant Christians have indeed tried to be nonconfrontational. Their goal has simply been to absorb violence without striking back. Their intent has not been to change the attacker.

While we want to recognize and respect this viewpoint, we believe careful examination suggests that even nonresistance is at least implicitly confrontational. As we hold up many examples of nonviolence and nonresistance, we will see that one thing characterizes both: they challenge another person to change, usually by confronting that person's way of seeing things and compelling choice.

Both methods ultimately confront persons with the need for new choices. Confrontation does not require force or violence and can be done in loving ways.

The definition of peacemaking varies widely in our society. The motto of the Strategic Air Command is "Peace is our profession." Police officers are commonly called "peace officers." Such terms imply that SAC members and police officers are professional peacemakers.

Jesus, in the sermon on the mount, says, "Blessed are the peacemakers, for they will be called children of God" (Matt. 5:9, NRSV). This is the only New Testament use of the word *peacemakers* (*eirēnopoioi*). Who makes peace? Only one place in the New Testament are we told of anyone making peace. In Colossians 1 we read:

> For God was pleased to have all his fullness dwell in him [Jesus], and through him to reconcile to himself all things, whether things on earth or things in heaven, by *making peace* [*eirēnopoiēsas*] through his blood, shed on the cross (Col. 1:19-20, emphasis added).

Biblical peacemaking is a process of reconciling someone to God. The Christian mandate is summarized by the apostle Paul.

> So from now on we regard no one from a worldly point of view. Though we once regarded Christ in this way, we do so no longer. Therefore, if anyone is in Christ, he is a new creation; the old has gone, the new has come! All this is from God, who reconciled us to himself through Christ and gave us the ministry of reconciliation: that God was reconciling the world to himself in Christ, not counting men's sins against them. And he has committed to us the message of reconciliation (2 Cor. 5:16-19).

This mandate might seem, at first glance, a call to preach the gospel in the usual evangelistic sense. It certainly is that—but it is also more. When conflict separates us from people, it separates us from God.

> Whoever says, "I am in the light," while hating a brother or sister, is still in the darkness. Whoever loves a brother or sister lives in the light, and in such a person there is no cause for stumbling. But

whoever hates another believer is in the darkness, walks in the darkness, and does not know the way to go, because the darkness has brought on blindness (1 John 2:9-11, NRSV).

When Jesus told the story of the good Samaritan, he made it clear that our brother is our neighbor, and our neighbor is the whole human race. As we allow hard feelings against people to separate us from them, we walk in darkness, separated from God. A peacemaker is one who takes the message of reconciliation to all who have separated themselves from God by separating themselves from other people.

The diagram below[3] shows the way that love of God, neighbor, and self are connected. The portion in the center where the three connect is the area of wholeness; in Hebrew it is called *shalom,* and we usually translate it as *peace.* When we push another person away or allow ourselves to be separated by conflict, we also separate ourselves from the wholeness of shalom that God intends for us. Only when our relationships with other people and with God are whole do we have the peace God desires for us.

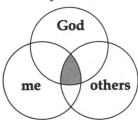

The peace we will be talking about in this book is not the absence of conflict. Peace is found where there is wholeness and fullness in relationships between people and with God. It is a dynamic situation where people struggle through real conflicts in ways which yield reconciliation rather than separation. People who work toward such relationships are making peace in a dangerous world.

Mapping the Approach

This *is* a dangerous world. Violence is all around us. It has become such a common part of the landscape that we scarcely notice it. One task for a person who wants to work toward peace is to learn to recognize violence. We will use stories to flesh out the difference between violence and nonviolence, as well as the concept of nonresistance as advocated by the historic peace churches.[4] The attempts at definition given above will begin to be meaningful through real situations.

Jesus calls us, not only to faithful thinking, but also to faithful action. This book asks what it means to *be* a faithful incarnation of the gospel. Faith, as we will be defining it here, is made flesh through deeds.

CHAPTER 2
The Politics of Violence

Violence. We recoil from the word and what it means to us. Being comfortable with violence is not socially acceptable in industrialized Western democracies. Part of the shock value of the punk and skinhead cultures of the late 1980s and the rap music of the 1990s is their acceptance of violence as normal. The mainstream American worldview of the twentieth century fears and rejects both violence and the hopelessness which usually accompanies it in cultures where violence is more common and acceptable.

Unfortunately, American culture is also obsessed with violence, as can be seen by watching television for a short time. The hypocrisy of teaching against violence while using it to sell products breeds a moral callousness which affects us all. When an American president feels his popularity slipping, a little military adventure in a place like Grenada or Panama or calling out the National Guard against drug smugglers can cause a quick surge of popularity. Then other things can be ignored.

We fear and reject the obvious and literal violence we see on the evening news. However, invisible, secret, threatened violence is built into every institution of our society, as we will now examine.

Systems of Social Control

Whenever someone uses a term like *social control*, we may think they are against government or against institutions in general.

That is not the case with me, and perhaps I should do a bit of confessing before we go on. I am a lawyer. Lawyers are, by definition, trained to work in the system. I am also a Mennonite pastor. Mennonite pastors are, by definition, committed to working in Mennonite institutions. I was an Air Force captain, trained to work in government and military institutions. I have created new institutions and re-organized old ones.

Training and experience have taught me much about the strengths and weaknesses of institutions. My task here is to share what I have learned.

The police are the most familiar institution of social control for most people.

> "911 dispatcher. Please state your emergency."
> "There's a man leaning against our fence. He isn't anyone from the neighborhood. Judging by his eyes, he's on something."
> "We'll have someone there shortly."
> In minutes two police cars arrived, and the man was taken away.

This real event occurred in a racially mixed neighborhood of average-priced, single-family homes in California. Both caller and dispatcher assumed without questions that a stranger, particularly a stranger under the influence of

some drug, was an unacceptable threat to the neighborhood. Caller and dispatcher did not discuss it, but both
knew that the police who came would use whatever force
was needed to remove the threat. They desired no personal contact by the caller with the strange man.

> "You are in violation of the temporary restraining order
> and are trespassing," stated the police lieutenant over a
> loudspeaker. "I urge you and I order you to disperse. . . . If
> you fail to leave, you will be arrested."
>
> The officer then explained the arrest procedures to the
> demonstrators and asked for their cooperation. The pro-
> testers continued to sing and chant slogans. Some block-
> ing the entrances to the building quietly left, but others
> took their places.
>
> Twenty-five officers armed with riot sticks began polite-
> ly arresting those blocking the doors, asking them to please
> walk quietly to the waiting buses.
>
> "We don't want to hurt our backs," said one of the offi-
> cers, smiling.
>
> Most complied with the request. Several demonstrators
> politely asked to be carried. Four officers carried each to
> the buses, which they boarded without incident.
>
> One man being carried began to scream and kick the of-
> ficers. He was handcuffed, shackled, and later charged with
> felony battery on a police officer.[1]

This protest, by Operation Rescue, shows how fine the
line is between overt (obvious or direct) and covert (con-
cealed or indirect) violence. On the one hand, police officers politely arrested equally polite and cooperative demonstrators for trespassing. On the other hand, they re-
strained a physically violent person who threatened their
safety. The water cannons and tear gas seen in televised reports of protests in other places were absent here—but
available.

When we think about it, we know that the police forces

of American cities are heavily armed, trained in the use of deadly force. This is a side of police duties seldom seen by the average person, except on television. There are many good reasons for a person to obey society's rules. But the fact remains: governments employ standing armies of law enforcement officers to make sure people conform. Most citizens call for more, not less, law enforcement.

Every time the legislature makes a new law, it states how the law will be enforced. It is up to the courts to decide how a law made by the legislature will be applied in particular situations. Every time a court applies the law to a situation, the police power of the state stands ready to enforce the court's decision.

The police forces of the United States can include National Guard troops and even regular Army troops on occasion, particularly in the face of large strikes or riots. While we may not like the term *social control*, we must recognize that these armed forces exist to make people behave in ways most people support. An attractive feature of democracy is that it allows more people to decide what behavior is acceptable, and courts to make fair decisions about people's behavior.

People usually see the judicial (justice) system in the United States and other Western countries as an alternative to violence. Letting a court decide your dispute is peaceful. A court decision certainly looks less violent than the old-fashioned blood feud. However, a court's decisions are meaningful only if the parties accept them, or if the court can enforce its decision.

Courtroom battles are as much battles as were the old trials by combat fought by champions for each side. The difference is that a courtroom battle looks nonviolent. Life and property are as much at stake in these quiet battles as they ever were in violent battles. But the violence is covert. It is silently threatened, rather than literal. It only becomes obvious when someone does not cooperate with the court or its decision.[2]

I talked to a bailiff (the sheriff in a courtroom responsible for the safety of judge and audience) who told me that divorce court was much more dangerous than criminal court. He took weapons away from people in divorce court more often than in criminal court.

The institutions of industrialized Western democracies all rely on the police power and judicial system of the nation to protect their property and operations and resolve their disputes. These institutions exist because such silently violent systems make it possible. Without police protection, institutions would hold property at great risk. A brief look at history shows that such institutions have only existed when protected by a strong central government or when powerful enough to protect themselves.

Churches, as property-owning institutions, are no exception. Some churches might prefer not to press charges when their facilities are burglarized, for instance. Yet they need a police report of the burglary to obtain insurance payments after a loss. Once the crime is reported, the criminal justice system handles it as any other burglary.

Churches are business organizations subject to the laws of governments. They are not exempt from usual government regulation of their business activities. When the church has exemption from some regulations or taxes, the exemptions are given by and administered by the government. Once a church becomes a property-owning institution, it is one more social institution made possible by the threat of violence underlying all government.

Historic peace churches have struggled from the beginning to separate church and state. They have seen many of their ideas on this separation become part of the democratic ideal. Even so, the freedom from government control which churches have in America and elsewhere is given them by the government. As with any gift, it can be taken away.

This happened recently in Arizona. Government agents infiltrated church organizations working to give sanctuary to Central American refugees and imprisoned the leaders of the organizations.

Freedom of religion, as far as government is concerned, is freedom to believe, not freedom to act. This has been true from the beginning of the free church five centuries ago. Churches which do things the government does not like have to consider whether doing them is worth giving up their tax exemption or even having their leaders imprisoned. We will talk more about the tax system below.

Courts and police are not the only systems of social control we have to deal with, although they underlie everything the government does. All government programs are, in some way, trying to control the lives of citizens. This is not necessarily bad, but it is the situation we live with.

The tax system, for instance, is designed to cause certain types of behavior. Certain things are tax deductible, others not. This encourages us to spend on deductible things. Some types of business investment or hiring policies get tax credits. This encourages businesses to operate in certain ways. Some years back, solar energy credits encouraged the development of the solar power industry—which could not get off the ground before the tax credits.

The tax system can be one of the more openly violent government programs. It seizes the property of people who do not pay their taxes and puts those who refuse to pay in jail.

The welfare system is designed to demand certain levels of effort from clients. It tries to build in incentives to finding a job. Of course, if everyone on welfare found jobs, there would be no jobs for welfare workers, so few real incentives are offered. The result is a situation where the minimal needs of welfare recipients are met while creating middle-class jobs for welfare workers.

This creates a permanent underclass of persons unlikely to escape poverty, but in whose name a vast bureaucracy emerges to extract tax money from citizens and administer its redistribution. Few people would cooperate with such a system without the threat of violence.

The education system is usually not thought of as a means of social control. But schools require attendance and tax money, which has a tremendous impact on how we see the world. Schools determine what behavior and style of dress are appropriate and what values will be taught.

Above all, they value conformity. Students learn not only reading, writing, and arithmetic. They learn also how to function within a bureaucracy, how to get along with authorities, and how to win at the "game" of school.

We don't think of the schools as being founded on violence. But if you don't show up, an officer comes and gets you. If you don't send your child to school, you can go to jail. Discipline at school can include corporal punishment, although these days a more modern view is to use only shame and guilt or the withdrawal of privileges to maintain discipline.

Violence exists in all areas of life.

They pulled a snap vote at the Sunday evening service and put that preacher in. I can't believe we were so gullible. He showed up here, and we needed someone to preach, so we let him do it, and then all these new people started coming and joining.

We didn't realize he had a church started and needed a building. Our regular attenders are outnumbered. We

have many members who weren't there that night. Maybe
we can reverse the vote.

The trouble is, they're probably going to have an election to replace the board this Sunday night. As soon as
they vote their people in, they'll vote the old members out.
Then they'll have our building. We need an injunction to
stop this election so we can get our people together.

This distressed church member is willing to use the judicial system in church affairs. An injunction is a court order to do or not do something. Here it would block an
election of new church board members so old members
could muster their forces and prevent a hostile takeover.
In this true story, the court did stop the election. It ordered
the church not to accept any new members until the matter could be decided in court. The church chose to obey.

When we look at styles of interpersonal relationships,
whether between family members, church members, or
other relationships within society, it becomes apparent
that covert violence forms the setting. No matter how loving parents are, for instance, they are larger than their children. They are able to restrain or punish them physically
until they are nearly grown. This sets up a power relationship based on the potential use of force.

Think of how our language projects this size difference
onto other relationships. We go to see the *big* boss. Employees are *sub*ordinates. Teachers work *under* a principal.
Lower courts are subject to review by *higher* courts.

For better or worse, violence is either actively or potentially involved in nearly every human relationship. If you
do me wrong, I can do something about it. The system pro-
tects me from you, at least in theory.

This can, of course, be either freeing or binding, depending on how I see it. If I assume the system could protect me from you, I can enter into a free and open relationship. On the other hand, if I think I will *need* the system to

protect me from you, I will relate to you in a guarded way, being sure always to preserve my rights.

If there is a trend in North American society on this point, it is toward greater protection of individual rights through guarded and examined relationships. Just as bankruptcy planning is now a part of setting up a new business, there is a trend toward divorce planning among those entering marriage.

"Protection of rights" may not seem like violent behavior. Usually it is not, in itself. Violence comes into the equation when we try to use or enforce those rights. If we use the judicial system to enforce the rights we have preserved, then the covert violence of the judicial system is called upon. If we do not plan to use the judicial system, then there is no reason to protect our rights in the first place.

The best personal protection is more likely to be found in open, transparent relationships which root out any confusion and deal with feelings as they arise. Persons who want to preserve their rights in a relationship will instead disguise their true feelings and only display those feelings and thoughts likely to benefit them.

The adversary system[3] used in American courts presumes this sort of guardedness. Unguarded comments made in the relationship can be used against a person in court. This is where the "get it in writing" mentality which pervades modern American life comes from.

People who enter a relationship believing they will eventually have to enforce their rights against the other person are constantly suspicious of the other's motives. This means that violence is the relationship's ultimate foundation.

The Roots of Violence

If violence is so ingrained in North American culture,

where does it come from? There are certainly many roots, some more important than others. One is described in the book of James.

> What causes fights and quarrels among you? Don't they come from your desires that battle within you? You want something but don't get it. You kill and covet, but you cannot have what you want. You quarrel and fight. You do not have, because you do not ask God. When you ask, you do not receive, because you ask with wrong motives, that you may spend what you get on your pleasures (James 4:1-3).

To have what we want, when we want it, is a desire that certainly causes many quarrels. The love of money is a root of all kinds of evil (1 Tim. 6:10), but it is certainly not *the* root of *all* evil. The desire to have power over another person is often the source of conflict.

In historic peace church circles, the problems caused by the desire for power have been recognized. A common result has been to create institutions where power is so diffused as to be invisible, even though this results in lower efficiency and a lack of leadership at times. The words of Jesus at the Last Supper are taken seriously.

> The kings of the Gentiles lord it over them; and those who exercise authority over them call themselves benefactors. But you are not to be like that. Instead, the greatest among you should be like the youngest, and the one who rules like the one who serves (Luke 22:25-26).

Power has been seen, in historic peace church circles, as inevitably corrupting. It is hard to find examples to prove otherwise. Persons who desire to be great cannot, by definition, love their neighbors as themselves. The peak of the pyramid has room for one.

Since a person who has power cannot be accountable to

anyone without sharing that power, a common result is a person who refuses accountability to anyone, including God. This view has resulted in a distaste for any hierarchy in historic peace church institutions. For a person to be above another is to risk violating Jesus' teaching about service to one another.

The desire for power may not, in theory, be inevitably corrupting. But it is safe to say that the desire to have power over other people is a root cause of violence.

Another root of violence has been identified by psychologists. Psychologists believe that the human body prepares for all emergencies in much the same way. When faced with a situation which might be a threat to our security, our bodies prepare for *fight* or *flight*. As we focus our attention on the threat, our breathing and heart rates decrease. This allows us to hold still, as if hiding. Our muscles tense, including our breathing muscles.

As we begin to run low on oxygen, our bodies respond by demanding adrenalin, to speed up the heart and breathing and to give our muscles increased strength. While all this is happening, our minds are analyzing the threat and deciding on a response. Depending on the situation and our understanding of it, we can label the same threat in many different ways, from danger to sexual arousal. Fascinating studies have demonstrated how this process operates.[4]

In modern life, we are not likely to be faced by a threat which literally requires either fight or flight. The low-grade anxiety caused by a confusing relationship at work causes the same physical response as the threat of a collision while driving. Neither offers an opportunity for the burst of physical exercise required to burn off the adrenalin produced.

The usual result is to view any confusing situation as producing anger and as requiring a fight or retreat. Our tendency to call this response to anxiety "anger" runs us headlong into our society's rule against expressing anger. This taboo is especially strong among Christians, who have often been taught not to express anger and even to deny that it exists.

I believe much of our culture's hidden violence can be attributed to this process. We fail to recognize what is happening inside of us and respond to any anxiety-producing situation as if to an enemy. At the same time, we believe it is wrong to feel this way.[5]

Any attempt to deal with our society's violence and to address conflict in helpful ways must examine these root causes. Solutions are needed which lower anxiety and produce those feelings of security and acceptance which allow peaceful resolution of conflict. That will be a goal as we look at alternative conflict resolution methods in the pages to come.

CHAPTER 3
The Theology of Violence

God the Angry Judge

Is God angry? In the Old Testament God is described as being angry over two hundred times! In the New Testament, not once. Jesus is angry one time (Mark 3:5). What is going on? Has God changed?

The Hebrew word most commonly translated into English as *anger* is *aph*. It is the word for face, nostrils, and anger. The image is clear when we see that God's anger is always being "kindled" or "waxing hot." What is being described are the physical effects by which a person's anger is shown—nostrils flare and tighten, the face reddens.

Greeks tended to see anger in more intellectual terms. The Greek word *orgē* means "excitement of the mind" and, by implication, anger. New Testament writers warn that certain behavior will make God angry, but never describe God's present state of mind, much less God's physical appearance.[1]

Greeks understood mental functions to be separate from other bodily functions. Hebrews, on the other hand, tended to see body and mind as a whole. While they knew that God transcends bodiliness, their language had no way to express emotions except as shown in the human body. Since the Greek view distinguished more clearly between emotions and bodily functions, it could describe emotional states without reference to the body.

We who grew up in Western cultures tend toward the Greek way of thinking. While the early church strove to translate the Hebrew God's ways into something understandable to Greek culture, we moderns tend to read the Old Testament through our Greek filter without pausing to ponder what we are doing.

We are often raised to consider bodily functions as inferior to our minds and their purer work. Emotions, which cloud the mind and have obvious physical effects, are to be avoided. That being the case, we tend to see all the Old Testament talk about God having emotions described in physical terms as quaint, primitive ignorance at work, thus to be ignored.

We wind up taking sides in this theological tangle. Some of us focus on the God we think the Old Testament shows us. This God's nostrils flare and burn with anger. Others of us focus on the soft, nurturant God we think the New Testament portrays. This God loves everyone and wants the best for them. Of course, when we put it that way, it is obvious that God is more than either of these descriptions. But we don't often put it that way.

Those who focus on God's anger tend to be impressed with the *law of talion* (*retaliation*, from Latin): "an eye for an eye, and a tooth for a tooth." God the righteous judge exacts perfect vengeance. There is symmetry in that sort of justice. It is noted less often that it was in God's mercy that this law was given as a substitute for the blood feud. This same "vengeful God" established cities of refuge for those who killed accidentally—and used a murderer, Moses, as a great prophet and leader.

Jesus sounds like someone changing God's direction when he says,

> You have heard that it was said, "An eye for an eye and a tooth for a tooth." But I say to you, Do not resist an evildoer. But if anyone strikes you on the right cheek, turn the other also; and if anyone wants to sue you and take your coat, give him your cloak as well (Matt. 5:38-40, NRSV).

Jesus said that he came not to set aside the law, but to fulfill it. In some ways, it seems that Jesus' teaching on not resisting evil persons is a basic change from the Old Testament. But, in fact, the whole sweep of the Old Testament is the story of God's purpose to establish a community of shalom for God's people.

Shalom *is* an extraordinarily rich Hebrew word. It describes a state of wholeness, fulfillment, and right relationships. It describes peace between peoples; plenty of food, water, and shelter; and spiritual oneness with God. What looks to us like a change between the Old Testament and the teaching of Jesus is really just the result of our limited vision for the fulfillment of the Old Testament promises.[2]

Shalom encompasses both a grace that nurtures and a wrath that insists on justice. A God without wrath could not be holy. A God who winks at sin would not be righteous. For God to be both holy and righteous, God must offer both grace and wrath.

When we ignore God's wrath, we deceive ourselves. In Matthew 25, Jesus tells the story of the sheep and the goats. The sheep are those who feed the hungry, clothe the naked, visit the sick and imprisoned. They are taken to be with God.

The goats are those who did not do those things. They

are sent to "the eternal fire prepared for the devil and his angels." God will set things right one day, and there is more to God's justice than mercy alone.

God is creating a people who share God's vision of shalom. Jesus announced the nearness of this "kingdom of God," saying it is both here and to come. The kingdom of God is present wherever people live in a state of wholeness with each other, God, and the earth. God the angry judge *and* merciful lover has been calling people to this vision for thousands of years. People who have this shalom vision strive to make peace in a dangerous world.

But what of those who do not have this shalom vision, those who care about justice seen as symmetrical vengeance? These people base their stand on the Bible, as do those who find no place for vengeance, even God's vengeance. Kelley Hayes tells this story about a demonstration in downtown Wichita, Kansas.

> Then a person came out of the bank. I don't know if he was a bank employee or what.
>
> He came out and said, "I fought in World War II, and I think you're a bunch of communists. I think you're godless. You're supporting godless communism. You don't know what you're doing. If you do know what you're doing, you're heathen, you're heretics, you're faithless people."
>
> He started at one end of the line of signs and talked to each person in a nose-to-nose way. Then he came to me and was saying these kinds of things to me. This person was really angry. I've never before faced anyone who was so crazy-acting. He was almost crying, just filled with emotion.
>
> I wasn't responding well. I tried to look him in the eye to see some of the hurt there. But mostly I sensed my own fear that this person might actually hit me. I didn't know what he might do, driven by such deep emotion.
>
> Finally he moved down and started talking to Mary Herron, the only woman there. I had a whole set of

thoughts like, What am I going to do if he becomes physically aggressive with her?

But I was impressed with Mary. Instead of having this male-to-male confrontation, she started saying things like, "I really hear you're hurting. I think you're really upset." She worked hard at letting him know that she could understand his feelings.

All the time he was saying, "You're just a godless person. You're Catholic. You know you should be saved. If you're a Catholic, you're probably not really a Christian."

When he was talking like that to me, a Mennonite, it was really confronting my faith. In some ways, I identified with his salvation and born-again language, but I believed the opposite of how he understood Jesus' message.

Mary was able to keep talking with him. The rest of us moved a little bit farther away because she was calming him.

Then finally Mary started saying things like, "Well, I disagree with you." He was starting to hear what she was saying. It must have been ten, fifteen minutes that she had been talking with him.

At the end, this man started backing off and saying good-bye. At that point we were able to talk to him and say, "We're glad you feel strongly about this, and we hope you can think about what's happening."

He didn't look nearly as angry when he left.

Mary Herron offered shalom, which included a grace that listened and nurtured as well as "wrath" that confronted the man with the truth. Those who have a shalom vision know that it is only through shalom living that others can begin to understand what the kingdom of God might look like here and now. As we offer ourselves to others, it must be in a way consistent with our understanding of shalom.

A Priesthood of Violence

Shortly after the American military involvement had ended in Vietnam, I was an air force legal officer assigned to a base in California. Among my duties was the defense of people charged with military crimes, acts which would not be crimes on the outside.

I was assigned to defend several people who were claiming conscientious objector status. One of the things I was surprised to discover in the air force regulations was a requirement that the base chaplain explain those biblical passages which seem to support participation in the military. The regulation was clearly aimed at talking "misinformed" persons into a more orthodox religious position consistent with military participation.

Political and religious authority have been linked throughout history. In primitive tribes, the chief and shaman share leadership. In the modern United States, the Congress has a chaplain, and presidents attend prayer breakfasts. George Washington noted that people without religion are ungovernable.

The underlying morality of religious heritage is what makes a modern, open society work. Throughout history, religion has been a particularly useful tool for governments in the control of uneducated masses. For that reason, governments have sought to control religion.

We discussed social control earlier. Here we return to it for a specific purpose—to examine what I call the "priesthood of violence" which serves modern states.

During the 1970s there was quite a bit of talk in historic peace church circles about "civil religion." It was a discussion of the kind of domesticated religion which exists in service of the modern industrial state. Of course, people don't want to see themselves as civil religionists. So the discussion ended with a lot of finger pointing and little confessing.

Believers church people need to be realistic in appraising their own stance toward government and how their religious understandings fit in with it. The believers church (a broad term for all those churches where membership is an adult decision rather than an accident of birth) began in reaction to government interference with the church.

In many ways, the early Anabaptists who defied the state by baptizing one another on confession of faith defined themselves in opposition to the state. In Zurich, Switzerland, where the first Anabaptists broke away from the established church, it was the city council who hired the town's preacher. Intermingling of church and state was nearly total. Ulrich Zwingli, the preacher of Zurich when the Anabaptists broke away, later died participating in a battle with Zurich's troops.

The situation in North America today is different. The radical Anabaptists' ideas about separation of church and state are the norm. While the military and the legislature have chaplains, most pastors have no connection to government. The government certainly does not pay them.

How, then, can it possibly be said that North America has a priesthood of violence? As has been pointed out earlier, Western democratic political systems presume a legislature which enacts laws, an executive which administers the laws, and a court system to balance the excesses of the other two branches of government.

When laws are enacted by the legislature, they include enforcement provisions. These enforcement provisions presume the existence of police power. Laws are intended to exert social control through subtle, or not so subtle, coercion, and to punish failure to comply. No matter how friendly legislation appears to be, the threat of violent enforcement underlies people's seemingly voluntary acceptance of these laws.

Religion in America has truly been a force for public

betterment. From the founding of America forward, preachers have inveighed against immorality which tears at the social fabric. They have applauded moral behavior which strengthens the social fabric.

Ideas such as strong families, care for the elderly and ill, abstinence from harmful substances, and honesty in business dealings have been the themes of religious involvement. Delayed gratification—suffering for the public good today in hopes of a bright eternity—has been a significant contribution of the church, encouraging people to look beyond self-interest. As Thomas Merton puts it in *No Man Is an Island*: "To consider persons and events and situations only in the light of their effect upon myself is to live on the doorstep of hell."

Public-spiritedness is a virtue which nearly requires a religious base. Materialistic countries commonly have to coerce such behavior by brute force or brainwashing techniques. Christians, on the other hand, willingly give up self-interest, at least to an extent.

The church, by opposing self-interest and promoting life-enhancing service to others, clearly serves the gospel message. Unfortunately, it also encourages, although not explicitly in most cases, respect for the status quo. It supports social service to bind up the wounds of victims of the government system rather than a more prophetic confrontation with the systems which wound.

By preaching respect for the government system and service within that system, the church sets up the system of government as a given, to be supported and honored. When the church establishes any given other than God, its loyalty is compromised. There can only be one given.

The heart of civil religion is the establishment of the existing system of government as a given. This makes it coequal with God.[3] This is exactly what happened to the European church in pre-Reformation times and to the German church as Hitler rose to power.

Religious people are unlikely to accept things which violate the basic tenets of their faith without the consent and encouragement of religious leaders. History demonstrates that there is little difficulty in finding such leaders. People minded to do something can usually find a religious leader to support their desires.

During the 1960s civil rights movement in the United States, churches were actively involved on both sides of the controversy. Pastors of these churches were able to speak out "prophetically" on both sides. Arguments honed in pulpits of the pre-Civil War South spread across the United States, as did abolitionist rhetoric of the same vintage.

To get a glimpse of how civil religion works we hear from Julie Lindorff, a member of Faith Mennonite Church in Minneapolis, Minnesota. She tells this story about her participation in a demonstration at the United States Capitol Building on Pentecost, 1981.

> We went into the rotunda and were in concentric circles. We began praying. It wasn't long before the chief of police came and spoke directly to Jim Wallis, the leader of our group. He gave three warnings.
>
> Each time Jim would just say, "No. We will not leave. We are here to let the nation and the Congress know that we don't want our tax dollars to go toward funding of the MX missile, which we believe to be against the very spirit upon which our country was founded."
>
> After that third warning, after Jim Wallis said, "No, by the Spirit of God we are here," it was like—BANG! Out of every door came about ten police officers. Tables went up. They lined the whole place with tables. They got the cords out and the big poles.
>
> Everybody went into action. There must have been fifty police officers there. It was so bizarre. It was like: "Oh, you

were ready for us, weren't you? Those paddy wagons were no joke!"

They started with the outside edge and worked their way in toward the middle. It was slow. We did a lot of singing and low-key reading of mostly the prophets and some psalms. It was a constant focusing, which was nice because the arrests took forever.

A police officer would come over, tap you on the shoulder and say, "I have to tell you that you're not allowed to pray in the rotunda of the Capitol, and I'll have to ask you to leave."

They had to do fingerprints, and the mug shot, all right there. We waited and waited and waited until we were picked off one by one. The first hour or two was spiritually energized and exciting. Toward the end it was a little bit tiring, wearing, and difficult.

I did a lot of internal conversation. It was hard to stay focused because of the anxiety and the people around. I tend to be introspective, and I probably wrote a whole journal that weekend. These images would come up. . . .

I would be there watching people being arrested and doing a little singing and trying to be still. And looking up and seeing a picture of George Washington and everybody signing the Declaration of Independence and thinking about the risks they took years ago.

Now we take the same kinds of risks, and it isn't okay with the government! I'm not the first to have these feelings. I'm not the first to want something better for my children. I'm in a long line of people for whom it's been a lifelong struggle.

When the status quo is accepted and the operations of a system of government are seen as givens, the violent coercion which underlies those systems is adopted as given.

As the Reformation began in sixteenth-century Europe, the Catholic clergy did their part to encourage the elimination of heretics. That is why the Protestant reformers who managed to gain acceptance by government quickly encouraged their government to eliminate those who wanted to push reforms further. Martin Luther was as hot to eliminate Anabaptists as Catholics had been to eliminate him!

The "magisterial" reformers were those who wanted changes in religious practices without any change in the relationship of church and state. They offered religious leadership which would support the government even more fully than the Catholic Church had. They were even willing to permit the government to seize Catholic Church properties. Thus they gained acceptance by the government.

Those who wanted separation of church and state would have to run and hide for many more years. They finally gained acceptance only when willing to buy peace with silence or to farm the frontier with small concessions from the government for their peculiar beliefs. Even in the young American colonies, religious toleration extended only to belief, not to practices opposed to government policy.

Church and State United to Control Society

Marilyn Miller grew up in Hesston, Kansas, in the Mennonite Church. She went to Hesston College and Bethel College, then taught school for five years. In the late 1970s she became involved in peace issues at Arvada (Colorado) Mennonite Church.

Active witness on peace issues became an important part of her ministry at Boulder Mennonite Church, where she served as pastor from 1984-1989. In August 1987, Marilyn participated in her first civil disobedience at Rocky Flats, the nuclear arms facility in the Denver-Boulder area. The nuclear bomb trigger production there was halted several hours through a nonviolent blockade by around 200 people. Marilyn tells the story.

> The sermon for that Sunday was based on Romans 8:28. "We know that in everything God works for good with those who love him, who are called according to his purpose [RSV]."[4]
>
> This doesn't mean that everything that happens is good, like the bombing at Hiroshima and Nagasaki. But God can make good come from it *with* those who love God. We don't just pray and God does it. God works *with* people to make good come from evil.
>
> On that Sunday there was a blockade of Rocky Flats. A lot of my friends had organized it and were working in it. I wanted to be there and support them, so early in the morning I went out with my daughter.
>
> The purpose was to put one's body on the road to stop the workers from going in. This stopped Rocky Flats from making bomb triggers for hours because it was difficult to enter unless one ran over the blockaders. It was the first time Rocky Flats had been successfully blockaded for so long.
>
> The blockaders were practicing what I was going to preach that morning. They were linking arms and trying to make peace. Some of the police were really hurting them— poking their eyes or bending their arms. The blockaders were giving themselves to make peace in the world.
>
> This said to me, "Hey, they're doing what I'm preaching about." I wanted to be a part of it.
>
> Yet I had a responsibility. I had to give a sermon at church that morning, so I went back. The office of the Rocky Mountain Peace Center, located in the church, was connected with a radio station so they could communicate what was going on.
>
> I told the peace office people that I'd been out at Rocky Flats. I said I would like to tell our congregation what was going on and encourage people to go out after church and join the witness.

They asked if they could call the radio station and other churches to announce that the Mennonite church was doing this. They wanted to ask other pastors if they would announce it in their churches, too.

I said, "Sure, go ahead."

In my sermon, I gave as an illustration what I had seen that morning. I told the people that I wanted to go out after the service and join these people.

Afterward, at least a half-dozen people from our church went out. They didn't cross the line, but they went out to support me. Two other people who crossed the line have become a part of our church since then.

It was clear to me that this was the right time for me to act, not that anybody else had to do it, but for me this was the right time. It was an expression of faith. It was saying, "Hey, what I'm talking about here I want to do with my life, not just with my words. I want to 'walk the talk.' "

I never had any hesitation or any fear. Maybe I thought, What's it going to cost? How much time is it going to take? Is it worth it? That kind of thing. But not much.

Most of the people had had nonviolence training and were connected in affinity groups. They would get arrested and then come back and block the road again.

The crowd was chanting, "The whole world is watching!" I knew that with this many people, the message was going to get around the world.

I wanted to add one more number so people could say, "Hey, there *are* people in the United States willing to go to prison for peace."

By the time we arrived, they had arrested all the people. There weren't any cars going into Rocky Flats at the west gate because of the blockade. So we went to the east gate, where there were about six people who wanted to blockade. We made our own affinity group.

We went over to the road. We saw that a car was going to come in. We all lay down on the road and hooked arms. We were across the whole road so they would have to run over us if they went in. The car stopped. The police came up and told us they would like us to get off.

We said, "We will stay where we are to stop the bomb-making and killing."

An officer read our rights and then two policemen picked me up. One took my feet and the other took my shoulders. They just pulled me up and carried me away.

I felt peaceful and right about it. I wasn't going to fight with them. But I wasn't going to move on my own. If they needed to move me, they could. I was doing what I could so we wouldn't have any more of those Hiroshimas and Nagasakis.

One of the arresting officers asked me, "Do you have any weapons?"

I answered, "The most powerful weapon in the world—a heart of love."

They frisked me and led me to a bus. I said to another officer, "Do you know how dangerous this is here, the pollution?"

He said, "Well, I used to live nearby in Broomfield, but I moved."

"Did you move because of the factory here?" I said.

He grinned. "I'm not allowed to answer."

But you could tell he had moved because he didn't feel it was safe for his health.[5]

Then they filled out their reports and released us. In the jury trial which followed several months later, I was found "not guilty" along with eleven others.

After the trial one juror thanked me for our witness and said, "Next time, I'll be out there, too."

A sense of rightness and peace has stayed with me and has not been shaken. I know there are a lot of Christians and religious people who don't think one should do this. But what I admire about the Anabaptists is that they were called to do what they thought the Scriptures and the Holy Spirit led them to do, not so much what everybody around them said.

From the Anabaptist tradition coming out of the Arvada Church and from being with the people in the Boulder

Church, I have received a conviction that peacemaking is a part of the Christian life.

And it's peace-*making*, which is more than peace-*loving*. There's a difference. Too many Mennonites see peace as just the absence of conflict. They don't want to stir up anything.

To me, in lasting peace, peacemaking, there often is conflict. You work through the conflict to come to better values and relationships than you had before. The older I get and the more involved I am with personal, church, or world issues, the more I'm not afraid of conflict and see the potential it has for awareness-raising and moral growth.

A core of people at Boulder Mennonite do not want to be a part of a church unless it is living the faith through participating in peace and justice activities. In the last two months, we have had four families come to the church because they heard that we were a peace church and were doing something about social issues. I see more and more that our mission is to be a church that takes seriously the peace stand, poverty, and injustice in the world.

I keep hearing how the possibility of a nuclear holocaust is effecting the morale and thinking of our children. Some feel helpless and hopeless.

Thus it was encouraging when a woman in the church called me the day after our action and reported her first-grade daughter's words: "Our church people went out to stop the bomb before the service, and our church people went out to stop the bomb after the service. People in our church *are* doing something."

What is wrong with this picture? While more and more church people, particularly priests and nuns, participate in demonstrations for peace and justice issues, most churches are not supporting such activities. Most major Protestant denominations have always had a "radical fringe" of pastors leading their congregations toward more active involvement in issues, but it was a fringe. Denominations which trace their roots to the Radical Reformation have always been somewhat more involved in activity related to peace and justice issues, but usually through organizations outside the church.

The institutional church has not believed that success and activism are linked. In one way the development of Christian Peacemaker Teams goes along with the usual history of activist movements within church institutions. Rather than have the institution itself involved in activism, it creates a new organization outside the institution for that task. This insulates the institution from risk.

In the very nature of the institutional church, we find the rub. Churches like the one Marilyn Miller pastored try to follow Christ in life. This is messy. Churches try this and that. They fail and succeed. People are renewed and backslide. People have sudden and strange enthusiasms; some of them continue and others evaporate.

As many such groups did their thing over the centuries, there were efforts to channel some of the inevitable excesses. The result was what we now call "the institutional church." This human creation tends to the deposit of revelation, encourages individual congregations, and disciplines those who stray too far from the path. It trains and certifies ministers to ensure their orthodoxy. It reacts against anything which does not fit established patterns.

Some would say that I have just described the creation of the Catholic Church, and that it is inappropriate to compare Protestant or Mennonite churches to it. After all, how can a group with congregational polity, meaning that each congregation is independent, have anything in common with the "institutional church" as I have described it?

For better or worse, Mennonites and other historic peace churches have come together in denominations and conferences for the same purposes the institutional church has always served. For our purposes here, there is no significant difference between historic peace church denominational structures and the thing I have called "the institutional church."

This built-in suspicion of anything new is a strength of the institutional church. It smoothes out the excesses of individuals and local congregations. It is also a chief weakness. It prevents the rapid change necessary for an organization to thrive in changing times. As the pace of change has increased, institutions have had more and more trouble adapting.

The result for the institutional church has been a loss of members, as fewer people value what it has to offer. Growth then often comes in messy, new congregations only lightly tied to the institutional church's way of doing things.

An institution is a large and slow-moving target. No matter how large the institution, governments with their violent, coercive power are able to control the institution's course. Those who successfully lead institutions are often those successful in dealing with the government. Success with government dealings means successful accommodation to the needs of government. The inevitable result is an institution which pursues its aims in ways acceptable to governing authorities. It is difficult for activists to thrive in such an atmosphere. The usual result is for activists to see little value in the institution.

Mennonite Central Committee (MCC), which does relief and development work all over the world, wanted to send school kits made by Mennonites to Vietnam. These kits contain small spiral notebooks, pencils, a ruler, an eraser and crayons in a drawstring bag. The United States government refused an export license, so MCC Canada handled the job. The government was obeyed, and the job was done.

Certainly this was a successful accommodation to each

other's needs. Yet it did nothing to right the injustice of the government denying such a humanitarian request. Church institutions tend to choose effectiveness over confrontation with government. The long-term goals of the institution are seen as served best by actions which push the government gently, if at all.

Messiness is not tolerated by government. Suppose you want the benefits of cooperation with the government, including tax exemption and freedom from other regulation, such as licensing of pastoral counselors. Then you must properly register with the government and maintain your activities within certain limits. The institutional church works to ensure that its individual congregations and employees do not jeopardize its status with the government.[6]

This may sound sinister, but as it happens it seems perfectly natural and sensible. An employee of the General Conference Mennonite Church asked the conference not to withhold federal income taxes from her paycheck, so that she could resist payment of taxes for war purposes. This resulted in an eight-year process of discernment within that institution.

As a historic peace church, the General Conference Mennonite Church has a firmly held belief that persons should not participate in war. As the nature of warfare changes, it becomes more clear that tax money can be of greater importance than personnel in modern warmaking. This led a growing group of people to be conscientiously opposed to paying the portion of their United States taxes (over half of every dollar) which go for war purposes.

Initially, the Division of Administration advised the General Board that failure to withhold income tax from the employee's paycheck would be a violation of the withholding law. Thus it should not be done. At triennial conference sessions in 1977, persons were nominated from the floor for the Division of Administration. Those who pledged to consider not withholding war taxes were elected over incumbents.

A search ensued for ways to grant the employee's request without subjecting the institution to risk. It was presumed that survival of the conference in its present form was a key value. One risk which concerned the conference was that congregations or individuals who disagreed with the employee's beliefs about war taxes might withdraw financial support if the church itself violated the withholding law. Another troubling risk was that the federal government might withdraw the conference's tax exempt status, levy fines, and imprison leaders.

None of these risks were to be taken lightly. Any would cause fundamental change in the conference, besides the personal risks to board members and key employees.

At the next triennial sessions, in 1980, the delegates were informed that no suitable way had been found to insulate the conference from risk. The delegates then instructed the board to use all "legal, administrative, and legislative" avenues to obtain exemption for the conference from the requirement of employer tax withholding.

At the triennial sessions in 1983, it was reported that all avenues for obtaining exemption were either closed or involved such long-term lobbying efforts as to be meaningless. The delegates then voted to instruct the board not to withhold income tax from those employees who so requested.

At this writing it has been seven years since the conference stopped withholding federal income tax from the wages of its employees who request this. The federal government has taken no action against the conference. The government has no difficulty collecting its taxes from the bank accounts of the employees, and it seems that another successful accommodation has taken place. When the gov-

ernment can meet its needs without violating the conscience of the institutional church, it does so.

This story is extraordinary in that a church institution
was able to make a decision to defy the government on an
important issue. That it took eight years of vigorous processing to get to that point shows how difficult it is to turn
an institution away from the path prescribed by government, even in areas where deeply held religious convictions are directly affected. This was truly a decision to follow God's will rather than Caesar's, and we can certainly
celebrate the fact that this particular institution was able to
change.

Church institutions, whether they intend to be or not,
are in an arrangement with government whereby the institutions behave in acceptable ways in exchange for favor-
able treatment.

Church institutions have even gone beyond that in re-
cent years. They are working actively with the government
to obtain laws regulating people's behavior. The most obvious effort is in trying to outlaw abortion, but there are
many smaller efforts aimed at gambling, alcohol and drug
use, nonmarital cohabitation, and sexual orientation.

If it is acceptable for the church to agree with governmental control of its own activities, why should it not seek
to use governmental power to enforce behaviors which
are "moral?" If the government can get the churches' support by passing legislation not harmful to the aims of government, why not do it?

The result is predictable, given world history. Since
chiefs and shamans first collaborated in the leadership of
tribes, politics and religion have made good bedfellows.
That is, so long as the aim of chiefs was the preservation of
the institution of chief, and the aim of shamans was the
preservation of the institution of shaman.

The preacher of Ecclesiastes was right—there is nothing

new under the sun. So long as church institutions are primarily concerned with their own comfortable existence, they pose no threat to the government, and the government is quite willing to help them.

The Sadducees had such an arrangement with the Roman government in Jesus' day. It served them well until that troublemaker from Galilee came along. Just as happened in Jesus' life, when people challenge the government, religious institutions tremble. Usually they do what they can to preserve the status quo. Part of the story of Christian Peacemaker Teams is how it tries to work with both church institutions and those who say church institutions have sold out to the government. We will see more of how that works.

CHAPTER 4
Saying "No" to Violence

Anabaptists Find Another Way

The historic peace churches trace their spiritual lineage to a group called Anabaptists who emerged from the Reformation of the sixteenth century.

Europe at the beginning of the sixteenth century was a continent in ferment. The New World had just been discovered. The printing press was making books available for the first time to large numbers of people. The Bible was becoming available in people's own language.

Perhaps more importantly, the Turks were on the move. The first thing printed by Gutenberg with a date (1454) warns of the Turkish menace, Constantinople having fallen to the Turks the preceding year.[1] With the fall of Constantinople came a flood of Christian refugees to Europe, including scholars bringing manuscripts of the Bible superior to those known in Europe.

As the Reformation began to take hold, violent persecution of religious dissenters also began. During this same period the Holy Roman emperor, Charles V, was at war against France. In 1527, he sacked Rome, confining Pope Clement VII, an ally of France. It is hard to separate political and religious interests during this time. Christians were fighting one another for control of Europe and the Vatican, while also fighting against the followers of Islam for the preservation of a Christian Europe.

These internal and external difficulties among Catholic leaders may well have been what allowed the Reformation to go forward. They perhaps prevented the various monarchs from presenting a united front against the reformers.

In 1530, the Catholic rulers reached a compromise and the Pope finally crowned Charles as Holy Roman emperor. He proceeded to work toward a peace which would heal the Protestant schism. But the reform had gone so far he was forced to accept it. In 1532, Charles recognized the Augsburg Confession in exchange for military assistance from the Protestant princes against the Turks.

Into this mix came the Anabaptists. Although various groups of Anabaptists eventually sprang up over Europe, the Swiss are generally considered the first. They began as young followers of the reformer of Zurich, Ulrich Zwingli. As they studied the Bible together and Zwingli preached week by week from the Greek New Testament, they came to convictions about necessary changes in the church and its ritual practices.

Zwingli, an employee of the council which governed Zurich, asked the council for permission to make each reform. The council generally gave it. The sticking point was the mass itself, which Zwingli and his group of followers found to be unscriptural. The council refused his request to discontinue the mass. Against the wishes of his followers, Zwingli agreed to this decision.

He also maintained the necessity of infant baptism, believing with Luther that all persons must be baptized members of the one church. Zwingli's young followers could find no scriptural basis for infant baptism.

The split between Zwingli and his followers came in January 1525, when three of them baptized one another on confession of faith, thus becoming Anabaptists (rebaptizers). These young men began to study the Scriptures even more intensely and to preach their views.

The movement spread rapidly. Baptism of adults and the voluntary church which that represented caused trouble. But one Anabaptist principle caused even more difficulty in that age of universal military service. This was the conviction that a Christian could not bear arms nor be involved in killing human beings, who were made in the image of God.

This refusal to bear arms extended to a refusal to participate in government service of any kind, since the government took human life for a variety of crimes. Furthermore, the Anabaptists could find no description in the Bible of a Christian magistrate. They decided to give the benefit of the doubt to God; they refused government service. It was not long before both Catholic and Lutheran magistrates were hunting down and killing Anabaptists.

It is hard for us to understand how radical it was in those days to suggest that there be a separation between church and state. The other reformers wanted to reform the church while maintaining its alliance with the state. For this reason they are referred to as "magisterial" reformers, those who maintained ties with the magistracy. There was no comprehension of any unfaithfulness in this arrangement, which the Christian church had enjoyed since the time of Constantine.

How was it that these Anabaptists found such a different vision for life in the same Bible the other reformers used? In many ways, the difference was the result of a fresh and naive reading of the Bible by these first Anabaptists. It was not customary for priests to study the Bible in those days. The result was that interpretations of the institutional church were handed down without challenge from one generation of priests to another.

The Anabaptists obtained the Scriptures and studied them with the intention of obeying what they could understand of them. This peculiar hermeneutic (method of interpretation) was a hallmark of the broader Anabaptist movement as it scattered over the face of Europe.

Anabaptists believed that private interpretation needed to submit to the group of believers. This prevented many excesses. Even so, the movement was messy. People came to widely divergent interpretations. There were even violent Anabaptists, who thought they needed to fight to bring in the kingdom of God.

The Swiss Brethren, as the descendants of those first Anabaptists in Zurich were called, held to their view that Christians were not to resist evil persons, and surely not by the use of weapons. They read Jesus' Sermon on the Mount (Matt. 5-7) as a collection of ordinary rules for daily living. Perhaps the most extraordinary teaching in that sermon is Matthew 5:38-45:

> You have heard that it was said, "An eye for eye, and a tooth for tooth." But I say to you, Do not resist an evil doer. But if anyone strikes you on the right cheek, turn the other also; and if anyone wants to sue you and take your coat, give your cloak as well; and if anyone forces you to go one mile, go also the second mile. Give to everyone who begs from you, and do not refuse anyone who wants to borrow from you. You have heard that it was said, "You shall your love neighbor and hate your enemy." But I say to you, Love your enemies and pray for those who persecute you, so that you may be children of your Father in heaven; for he makes his sun rise on the evil and on the good, and sends rain on the righteous and on the unrighteous (NRSV).

The Swiss Brethren took the ideas of cheek turning and

enemy loving literally. They could not figure out how to love someone and kill them at the same time. So they rejected physical violence. Luther had gotten around this passage by separating the public duty of persons required to enforce the law from the private duty of Christians to love their enemies. Anabaptists refused to follow Luther's dualistic path.

Many people have tried to dilute or explain away the force of these words of Jesus over the years. But the descendants of the Anabaptists have tended to take them literally at most times and places since about 1560. The intense persecution suffered by the Anabaptists weeded out those who would fight. They were killed, while those who ran away found refuge.

By 1560, when Menno Simons worked to gather the ravaged remnant of Anabaptism in northern Europe, the view of the Swiss Brethren that Jesus' words were to be taken literally had won out. Called the principle of nonresistance, this view became foundational for the groups which came to be known as the historic peace churches.[2]

Mennonites and Brethren rose directly from these Anabaptist groups, with Quakers coming by another path later on. From here on I will focus on the Mennonite development of the doctrine of nonresistance in America. Much will be in common with Brethren and Quakers, but not all.

As I have mentioned, Anabaptism was a messy movement. It sprang up all over Europe in a very short time and was quite different in different places. The understandings of those called the Swiss Brethren had a strong influence on modern Mennonites. For that reason we will pay most attention to their particular stream of Anabaptism rather than the many others which rose simultaneously.

As Anabaptists congregated where they were tolerated, mostly in the Netherlands by 1700, they bought their peace with silence. They became *die Stillen im Lande*, the quiet in the land.

The principle of nonresistance served them well. It slowly crystallized into a way of life with a distinctive approach to human relationships. A quiet, firm honesty was prized, as well as a certain transparency of personality by which a person's true feelings could be seen in behavior and speech.

Since greed led to strife, and since materialism and greed were linked, both were frowned on. "Worldliness," defined as "keeping up with the Joneses"—or having things your Christian brothers and sisters did not—was to be avoided.

An interesting sidelight comes with the beginning of Anabaptist migration to the New World. In 1700 there were twenty-five Mennonites in America. They lived in Germantown, Pennsylvania, the first of thousands who would come. The desire to maintain distinctive communities where nonresistance was prized led those who most believed in these separatist principles to emigrate to America in groups.

The result was that those who stayed in Europe, mostly in the Netherlands, began to assimilate into the culture around them. Meanwhile, those who went to America formed communities of like-minded people.

As the leaders who prized nonconformity to the world left the country, it became easier to be more like the neighbors. In the end, Mennonite distinctives weakened in Europe. They were reintroduced after World War II by mission workers from North America. My wife's ancestral church in a Mennonite village in Germany has a large plaque in the sanctuary listing members killed while serving in the German Army in World War II.

By steadily eliminating many of the strivings which caused conflict and by their strong sense of community, Mennonites in America began to insulate themselves from the world. As their practices became more peculiar in comparison to people around them, they related less to people in the larger world. Mennonite groups became virtually closed communities.

In these closed communities, nonresistance came to have a technical meaning. As society became more civilized, the issue of killing became less significant, except in wartime. By holding themselves aloof from the people around them, Mennonites did not participate in government. Thus their holding of offices or jobs where law enforcement was involved ceased to be an issue. Using the courts was forbidden by the Mennonite churches. However, since Mennonites tended to do business with each other and church discipline took care of the usual trade disputes, it was not a frequent issue.

The term *nonresistance* fell into disuse. It was replaced by a stoic refusal to use violent or coercive means, outside of church discipline. *Coercive* came to mean any attempt to force a person to do anything by any means. The pacifism of nonresistance became a kind of passivism in personal affairs.

It was not until the middle of this century that the term *nonresistance* was again used with vigor. Guy F. Hershberger revitalized it in his 1944 book, *War, Peace, and Nonresistance.*[3] The concept of nonparticipation in the military had been addressed at the start of both world wars. Mennonites and related groups, such as the Society of Friends, gained conscientious objector status for men who were conscientiously opposed to participation in any war.

This was not based on nonresistance itself. It was rooted in the principle of conscientious opposition to participation in warfare—which is only a small portion of the territory covered by the principle of nonresistance.

In *The Politics of Conscience,*[4] a book describing the process by which Mennonites and others resisted participation in the two world wars, Keim and Stoltzfus describe the "thoroughgoing pacifism" of some groups such as the Mennonites. This pacifism may have been broader than nonparticipation in warfare. However, other aspects of nonresistance were not sufficiently important to the immediate issues to merit much discussion in the writings of the time.

The typical personal application used by draft boards was to ask a draftee claiming CO status whether he would use force to protect himself or a loved one from attack. A "yes" answer was a sure ticket into uniform.

Not until World War II was nearly over did Hershberger's book appear. It broadened the definition of nonresistance and carefully compared it to the various types of pacifism abroad in the land. Hershberger took Reinhold Niebuhr to task for his dualistic separation of New Testament nonresistance. Niebuhr saw nonresistance as a witness to the pure Christian ethic—but also saw a role for Christian militarism as the necessary solution to the current political order.

Hershberger plainly showed that Mennonites followed a covenant theology by which the moral law of the Old Testament was interpreted and fulfilled by Jesus in the new covenant. He explained the Mennonite view as finding in Jesus the authoritative interpreter of God's will for humankind.

Hershberger issued a call to nonresistant renewal. In the next section we will examine how that call came to be interpreted by postwar Mennonites. We will also suggest ways it might be interpreted at the end of the twentieth century.

Theology Without Violence

Theology has been so interwoven with violence throughout Christian history that it is difficult to imagine what it might look like without violence. Can the biblical theology of shalom become reality in our lives without violence to maintain the peace?

A story may help. This story is from Charles Walker who, as organizer of Friendly Presence, was active in Philadelphia in 1982 when this action took place. Walker is a member of the Society of Friends.

> The truck came soon after 8:30 a.m. The contract said to haul away to storage the possessions of the McDaniels family, on Conlyn Street in North Philadelphia. The house had been taken over by the Veterans Administration [VA] after Mr. McDaniels lost his job and couldn't keep up the monthly payments. The factory where he worked had closed.
>
> When the family tried to talk to the VA after they had come up with some money, they were stonewalled. The VA took a hard line, as it had been doing for some time, and said nothing could be done about it.
>
> To make matters worse, the family would be charged for the hauling and storage, usually about $30 a week. The bills would keep piling up and the emotional burden become heavier, because the family wanted to hold on to its belongings, especially prized items accumulated over a long period of time.
>
> "Come help the McDaniels save their house! You could be next!" The message came out over a bullhorn, addressed to neighbors and passersby.
>
> The movers were faced with a phalanx of over twenty people with signs, filling up the steps and porch. Some were neighbors supporting the family. Others were organizational people working with the Foreclosures Crisis Campaign. Expressions on faces were calm, determined. I imagined Richard Attenborough would have been proud to have them in his Gandhi film.
>
> Apprehensive folk, such as the truck driver and movers, apparently saw them as threatening (the truck group was

all white) and felt that to take on this group would have been dangerous. I saw the peace brigaders as displaying nonviolent strength.

The movers called the sheriff. When the sheriff arrived and we passed on the street, he asked me if I was from the VA office, maybe because I'm white and wore a hat. The crowd looked at me suspiciously until I was introduced as "from the Friends."

The sheriff's office has been outspoken against throwing people out on the street. Though the public doesn't know it, some judges are quietly collaborating and granting postponements, all hoping some new development will change the picture. One sheriff in Johnstown was jailed when he refused to evict a family.

Sheriff O'Donnell sized up the situation and talked to Kathy Fitzgerald, the effective young Jesuit volunteer who organized the event. She explained why they were there: the VA did have other options but wouldn't talk, they couldn't and shouldn't have to demonstrate every time there was a tough foreclosure, and the VA should get the message—negotiate.

At one point the sheriff asked, "Where are the McDaniels?"

She shrugged and smiled disarmingly. He repeated the question and got the same noncommittal response.

He smiled and turned away jokingly. He had "tried," perhaps to forestall potential critics on the scene, press included, who might have accused him of collusion with the demonstrators.

A few weeks before, in West Philadelphia, there had been more edge to the tension. The writ server came but didn't try to buck the crowd, about forty people that time. He called the police; they came, but never got out of their car.

This time at the McDaniels', the police did not even come. The sheriff may have assured potential police callers that things were under control. He called the VA office, apparently the second time, and asked someone to come to the house. Soon a black woman in her thirties arrived via slow deliberate walk, and negotiations began.

And that was the whole point of the confrontation! The action was designed, not only to head off the removing of McDaniels' possessions, but also to move the VA office off of its unbending line. The VA has other options not well publicized:

1. lease the house back to the McDaniels family,
2. arrange some combination of lease-purchase,
3. negotiate a compassionate arrangement,
4. pick up the mortgage themselves.

Finally, after negotiations on the street and on the phone, someone in City Hall had to be called to okay the proposed deal, which would postpone legal action for a month while other options would be explored.

"Don't leave until that truck has really gone. You don't know what they'll do," co-organizer Horace Small cautioned.

A man in our group said he worked for a moving company one time. He wouldn't be surprised if they went out of sight long enough for the group to dissolve, then returned for the original pickup. We stayed. The sheriff finally announced the postponement, subject to signing some papers.

It is an interesting commentary that our world is so full of violence that nonviolent presence is feared as a threat of violence, rather than as a moral challenge. What set the sixteenth-century Anabaptists apart was their theology of nonresistance—a theology without violence. As we discussed earlier, the God of both Catholics and Protestants during that period was a God of vengeance. This God was to be pacified by good works and sacraments, if you were Catholic. If you were a Protestant, this same God had a storehouse of grace for you to receive in fear and trembling.

Anabaptists instead saw God as wanting all creatures to

live a life of wholeness, shalom, in which the causes of
strife were undone in a community of righteousness based
on the love shown by Jesus. This was a shift of major pro-
portions. It was what allowed Anabaptists to calmly accept
death by torture, knowing that they were safe in God's
love. The *Martyrs Mirror* contains the testimonies of many
such people.

Some have said that *Anabaptist theology* is an *oxymoron* (a
term that contradicts itself), like *clever idiot*. Anabaptists did
not produce much written theology to explain their views
of God. They were action oriented. Their theology needs
to be inferred from their behavior rather than read in their
books.

Those who followed the understanding of the Swiss
Brethren were consistent in their actions and testimony on
nonresistance. They understood Christ to call for truth-
telling and nonresistance to persecutors. This meant that,
when caught, they would not deny their beliefs or attempt
to defend themselves physically in ways which would
harm their persecutors.

Anabaptists also understood God to have established
the ruling authorities (Rom. 13). It would be fighting
against God to fight against the authorities. This did not
preclude testifying to the truth of the gospel and vigorous-
ly defending themselves in disputations. But it did preclude using violence in their own defense.

Anabaptists were regularly ordered to cease preaching
and to leave a prince's domains, only to be later caught
preaching in the same place. Submission to ruling authorities did not include obeying them. It meant only accepting
the punishment the rulers meted out.

This point cannot be overstressed. John Howard Yoder
and Walter Wink have both written ably on it; we only
need sum up this critical understanding here. Romans 13
calls for submission to the ruling authorities, just as

Ephesians 5:21 calls for mutual submission out of reverence for Christ.

Submission does not mean *obedience*. One who is subject to the ruling authorities recognizes their ability to require obedience or punishment, but not their right to determine God's will for an individual believer. Were this not true, there would be no Mennonites or any other free church.

By its very existence, the believers church denies that submission to the ruling authorities requires obedience to them.

As the apostles said to the Sanhedrin in Acts 4:19, "Judge for yourselves whether it is right in God's sight to obey you rather than God."

What happens when a congregation is asked to support an act of civil disobedience? In 1982, Faith Mennonite Church in Minneapolis was faced with this question. Two members, Frank Trnka and Troy Couillard, were involved with the Honeywell Project, a group of community people who continue to hold vigils Wednesday mornings to protest Honeywell's arms production. The company is known for its manufacture of cluster bombs and components for the MX missile and Trident submarines.

When the Honeywell Project planned a mass demonstration which might include arrest for those participating, Frank and Troy came to the congregation requesting support for their participation. Pastor Myron Schrag tells how the congregation received teaching on the issue, worked through decision making, and followed up with special services after the action.

> A congregational meeting was called for a Sunday evening to consider Frank and Troy's request for support. That Sunday morning the sermon topic was civil disobedience. A part of the sermon was the presentation of several skits from Anabaptist history where people chose to obey God rather than earthly authority.
>
> I took a couple of stories out of *Martyrs Mirror* and wrote

them up as skits. They had to do with people disobeying the magistrate to obey Scripture. The sermon was simply about discipleship. My text was the Acts passage where Peter said "obey God rather than men."

This set the stage for the evening meeting. Several of the organizers from the Honeywell Project were present. They were thrilled and amazed that a church would even take time to discuss the issue and have fifty people out to talk about it.

It soon became apparent that most of the people were sympathetic to Frank and Troy's request. The initial reaction was not the question of civil disobedience itself, but how civil disobedience could convey a Christian witness.

The congregation gave several suggestions as to which kinds of acts could be supported and which would create difficulties for them. There was a strong feeling that the congregation would not support the destruction of property or the pouring of blood. They would support peaceful symbolic actions such as sharing bread or giving personal testimonies as to why our people were involved.

In this case we agreed to work by consensus. I give a lot of credit to our congregational moderator for being very sensitive in leading us through that. It would have been a potentially divisive issue had we taken a straight vote. But we wanted everyone to have a say.

The process took a long time because people worked diligently and with some difficulty. In fact, the meeting had to be recessed and reconvened before consensus was achieved.

Some members objected to supporting civil disobedience until all possible legal alternatives had been exhausted. Others pointed out that other unjust laws and causes were changed only after civil disobedience drew attention to them.

The congregation agreed to five actions:

1. A leaflet stating the following would be distributed at the demonstration: "Troy Couillard and Frank Trnka of the Faith Mennonite congregation have decided to participate

in today's action of Holy Obedience. In the spirit of our strong heritage as an historic peace church, we offer our prayers, our presence, and our financial resources." (Financial resources meant paying bail money if that was necessary.)

The brief statement concluded with the words of Jesus: "How blest are those who hunger and thirst to see justice prevail. They shall be satisfied."

2. The congregation would contribute $100.00 toward the leafletting of Honeywell plants upon approval of the contents of the leaflet by church representatives.

3. The church would send a letter to Edson Spencer, chairman of the board of Honeywell, with copies to the Honeywell board and local political figures.

4. The congregation would set aside time at a future church gathering to have an "offering of letters" written by individuals to Edson Spencer and the board of directors of Honeywell.

5. The congregation would have a banner at the rally.

The whole process of discernment did much to strengthen the congregation and bring it closer together. It must be said that a couple of families were uncomfortable with having the church even discuss the issue. They drifted away from the church.

On the other hand, many saw this openness, acceptance, and willingness to tackle tough issues. It attracted new people, and we gained more than we lost.

One fellow, who was really quite conservative, said, "Some people see their calling as going to Africa. It's not something I would do, but I can certainly support it. Others see their calling as going to Honeywell. It's not something that I would do, but as a Christian brother I can affirm them doing that." We were able to develop that kind of a spirit.

About seventeen people from Faith Church were present at the demonstration. Some provided music. At the suggestion of the Faith Mennonite congregation, bread was distributed at the rally. Those who planned to be arrested were asked to give personal statements on why they felt it was important for them to risk arrest. Many of the participants spoke from a faith perspective and some from a humanist perspective.

The rally was peaceful and nonviolent in every way. Several rally organizers gave credit to the Mennonites for keeping it nonviolent. The group was not allowed to enter the Honeywell building nor did Edson Spencer meet with them as requested. Some demonstrators stayed on the Honeywell premises all night. The next morning thirty-five people were arrested, including Frank. All were released without bail.

Later we sponsored two simple services on site. One was on a Sunday afternoon at Honeywell headquarters. Other people came, not just our people. We sang some peace songs and had some readings, both from Scripture and from other sources.

Then one weekday around noon we had a service at a manufacturing plant in north Minneapolis where all they do is fulfill defense contracts. We had a procession where we carried a cross. We sang songs and had readings.

A fellow who worked there was a neighbor of one of the women involved in the procession. He saw her and came over.

"What are you doing?" he asked.

"We're having a little worship service here for peace," she said.

"Mind if I join you?"

"Not at all."

He joined right in and said, "I don't like to work here. I need a job, but I don't like what I'm doing."

* * *

I think we're called to be prophetic, to take some risks, and not to compromise. But I think we've lost some of that vision in a lot of our churches. Many of us won't even talk about such issues as civil disobedience. People won't take the time to study the material the church puts out. You wonder how alive churches which don't tackle controversial issues can be. That's what the faith is about—taking risks.

It's part of our history. The Anabaptists were always taking risks. That's what got them in trouble. We only became the "quiet in the land" when we got tired of all the persecution. But the Anabaptist movement originally was bold. The Honeywell Project has helped me as an ethnic Mennonite to better appreciate my own heritage and what Anabaptist theology is all about.

CHAPTER 5

Personality, Violence, and Nonviolence

An Anabaptist Theory of Personality

How can we come to an understanding of sixteenth-century Anabaptist theological anthropology (how God works in humankind)? Anabaptists did not write down an explicit personality theory. As with the Old Testament, we must unearth the implicit personality theory which underlies Anabaptist thought. The core beliefs of Anabaptists are the place to find clues to their personality theory. I believe *discipleship* is the area of thought which best demonstrates this implicit theory.

When we study old views of discipleship we discover that we are shaped unknowingly by our predecessors. If we do not understand how they looked at the work of God in humankind, we can bless beliefs and practices which, while speaking to their situation, are out of line with our other beliefs, never realizing we have done so.

The Core Beliefs of Sixteenth-Century Anabaptist Theological Anthropology[1]

1. Humankind is saved by God's grace.
2. Each person makes a free choice for or against Christ.
2. Predestination is rejected.
3. God and human beings work together for human salvation.
5. Cross mysticism: the work of Christ on the cross is a mystery which we glory in, but do not explain.
6. General revelation prepares people for the message of salvation.
7. Works of faith are part of faith.
8. Justification is by obedience.
9. Sanctification is by obedience.

This list of nine core beliefs could be boiled down to two items: God's grace, and humankind's faithful response. It is not surprising that Anabaptists spent their energy defining and discussing the human response to God's grace rather than the gift of grace. The latter was a given, particularly in light of the Anabaptist view that the Catholic church of their day was not trying to seriously follow Christ.

In this way discipleship, following after Jesus' example, became the key Anabaptist criterion for describing a life of faith. The book of James spoke to this situation, describing the emptiness of a life without works of faith.

It is significant that Luther disregarded James, calling it a "straw epistle." His *simul justus et peccatur* (at the same time justified and a sinner) was rejected by Anabaptists, who believed that each person had the ability to choose whether or not to sin. Sin was, for the Anabaptists, a moral rather than an ontological category. This simply means that we are not doomed by our very existence to sin.

This brief survey of the core beliefs of sixteenth-century

Anabaptism shows a preponderance of interest in the area of action which demonstrates a saving faith. Faith and right actions are inextricably interwoven in sixteenth-century Anabaptist thought and together form the core of Anabaptist belief.

It is no less confusing to discuss the link between faith and action today than it was in the sixteenth century. Today we have the added confusion brought by modern psychology, which says that seemingly good behavior can be a symptom of sickness. The explosive growth of twelve-step, self-help groups for co-dependents suggests many are finding that good behavior is for them a mask for unhealthy ways of relating to people.

The Anabaptist understanding of personality seemed naive when it arose and seems so today for different reasons. Let us examine it with open minds to see what we find.

The Implicit Anabaptist Personality Theory

1. People are created good.

In opposition to the magisterial reformers who said people were born in sin, the Anabaptists affirmed the goodness and innocence of persons at birth. Innocence continues until the age of reason. Then people have the capacity to choose other than the good. People do inherit an inclination to sin, and sin is nearly inevitable. Only Jesus avoided all sin.

2. People can change.

To oversimplify, perhaps, the magisterial reformers generally accepted a view of humankind which trapped people in an inherent sinfulness. Original sin was transmitted in a biological way to new generations; sin was an inevitable part of being human.

Anabaptists generally acknowledged the likelihood of sin, but resolutely maintained the possibility of sinlessness. As C.J. Dyck said, "Historically sin is a condition of humankind, but existentially it is an act of will, a rebellion against God deliberately carried out."[2] Regeneration took away the desire to sin. It then lay within the person's power to choose the way of perfection, even as Christ did.

Both Menno Simons and Dirk Philips, considered by many the principal architects of the Anabaptism which has come down to us, had largely traditional views of Creation and Fall. They saw humans as having a dual nature, created in God's image for eternal life, but corrupted by transgressions. The Fall was a result of willful disobedience. This disobedience did leave humankind with the knowledge gained through disobedience. But it cost them; they lost their original purity. Simons and Philips believed that God made provision for a restoration of the likeness to God.

An important difference between Anabaptists and magisterial reformers was their understanding of Christ's work on the cross. To the Anabaptists, Christ, through his obedience and death, had freed all humanity from the stain of original sin. To deny this would be to say that the sin of the first Adam was stronger than the grace of the second Adam, Jesus Christ.[3]

Menno and Dirk did not have a traditional view of original sin. They did believe, however, that the original disobedience left humans with a tendency to sin. Dirk observes that all became sinners. Menno and Dirk both believed this tendency to sin was somehow inherited but not counted as sin unless one follows that influence and does sinful works.[4]

Menno expressly rejected Zwingli's views of predestination. That would make God responsible for sin and evil, rather than humankind.[5] Along with this rejection of predestination came a rejection of the doctrine of total depravity and the infant baptism made necessary by it. Ana-

baptists were consistent in saying that children were inno-
cent. They could not accept the idea that God would damn
a child just because baptism had not taken place. They
considered this contrary to all scriptural evidence.[6]

These views on children and sin do not come from sen-
timentality or a humanistic optimism. They come rather
from the understanding that Christ's work has undone the
sin of Adam and Eve. This is God's grace and forgiveness.[7]

The necessary corollary to this position, which has already been discussed above, is that people who sin can repent and turn back to God. Sin is, in Anabaptist thought, a
behavioral/moral category. As Friedmann says, "Ever
since the days of the apostolic church, Anabaptism is the
only example in church history of an 'existential Christianity' where there existed no basic split between faith and
life. . . ."[8]

The idea of sinlessness being possible sounds ridiculous to us, and the sixteenth-century Anabaptists did not
suggest that they achieved it. It is probably more accurate
to say that they saw sinlessness as a goal of faith toward
which we move. Christ's work on the cross makes it possible for us to avoid sin, but our sinful nature and the sin of
the world around us makes it difficult to avoid sin.

On the other hand, what other goal could one want? To
say that a sinless life is simply impossible is to admit defeat
before beginning. The Anabaptists wanted to be sure to
value Christ's saving work above all and to claim it by living a life faithful to Christ. That is neither overly simplistic
nor unrealistic.

*3. Through belief in God and obedience to God's commands,
people participate in the divine nature.*

God provides the power of obedience through grace,
but people must choose to use that power. Simply stated,
God would not ask for an impossible obedience. Obedience is, therefore, to exercise humankind's free will. When

persons are regenerate and live according to the will of God, Christ lives in them and they in Christ.[9]

This understanding came from various passages in the Bible. It is supported by Jesus in John 14:23, NRSV: "Those who love me will keep my word, and my Father will love them, and we will come to them and make our home with them."

Second Peter 1:3-4 says:

> His divine power has given us everything we need for life and godliness through our knowledge of him who called us by his own glory and goodness. Through these he has given us his very great and precious promises, so that through them you may participate in the divine nature and escape the corruption in the world caused by evil desires.

This mystical relationship is at the heart of Anabaptist belief. The person is made up of body, soul, and spirit. Even though creatureliness and sin separate the body and soul from God, the spirit remains connected and able to lead the person to regeneration.[10]

Regeneration is a term which describes repentance, conversion, and the continuing process by which God's grace transforms the very nature of the believer.[11] This power is as active today as in the sixteenth century. Talking about it probably sounded as out-of-step then as it does now. The simple understanding of God's promises is what set Anabaptists apart in the beginning, and it continues to do so today.

4. Personality is truly shown by behavior.

A person cannot be a secret Christian, because Christian love can only exist as it is openly shown. Where Christian love is not demonstrated, it does not exist.[12] These principles were peculiar to the Anabaptists. Simply put, a Christian was to be transparent. Their yes was yes, their no, no.

If there was goodness in their hearts, they would exhibit it. If there was hatred in their hearts, that too would show. Sixteenth-century Anabaptist hunters discovered this to be a true mark of the Anabaptist. They would ask suspects if they were Anabaptist; if they were, they admitted it. The *Martyrs Mirror* is replete with such stories.

Menno and Dirk both taught that the beginning of salvation is not confession of sin, as Luther would have it, but repentance and reformation of life. As Menno said, "If you do not repent there is nothing in heaven or on earth that can help you. . . ."[13] ·

Leaving aside the question of whether God can grant salvation to the unrepentant, it is clear that Menno understood actual change of life to be the key to salvation. He presumed such a life change to be accompanied by a change of heart. Neither would be effective by itself.

Faith is shown by works. The individual is to be transparent, exhibiting the true self in outward action.

> The regenerate, therefore, lead a penitent and new life, for they are renewed in Christ and have received a new heart and spirit. Once they were earthly-minded, now heavenly; once they were carnal, now spiritual; once they were unrighteous, now righteous; once they were evil, now good, and they live no longer after the old corrupted nature of the first earthly Adam, but after the new upright nature of the new and heavenly Adam, Christ Jesus, even as Paul says: Nevertheless, I live; yet not I, but Christ liveth in me.[14]

How Is This Anabaptist Personality Theory Compatible with Modern Mennonite Views?

1. Discipleship then and now.

We began by saying that discipleship is the category best suited for uncovering implicit Anabaptist personality theory. That is true, so long as we separate sixteenth-century definitions of discipleship from modern ones. Not mentioned above, since it is not an aspect of personality theory, was the Anabaptist view that discipleship would inevitably lead to suffering, even martyrdom. As with most Anabaptist beliefs, this one was discovered empirically. Anabaptists didn't sit in studies and think up the idea of suffering as a necessary part of discipleship. It simply emerged.

The idea first appears in incipient Anabaptist writings in Conrad Grebel's letter to Thomas Muntzer, dated four and a half months before the first adult baptisms.

> True Christian believers are sheep among wolves, sheep for the slaughter; they must be baptized in anguish and affliction, tribulation, persecution, suffering, and death; they must be tried with fire. . . .[15]

While no one had been martyred yet, the direction events were headed was clear to Grebel as he wrote. The course of events shows well in *The Sources of Swiss Anabaptism*.[16] Much water had passed under the bridge, and Grebel saw that a break with Zwingli's reform could only result in suffering for the rebels.

Modern views of discipleship are rather different. In the sixteenth century it was treason punishable by death to join the Anabaptists. While being a member of the Mennonite mainstream can be difficult for a politician or police officer today in the industrialized west, few other professions create much conflict with Mennonite beliefs. At times it is inconvenient to be a conscientious objector to military participation, but not most of the time.

For sixteenth-century Anabaptists discipleship meant regeneration—repentance, turning from sinful life, the beginning of a life which mirrored Christ's. It meant separating oneself from much of one's cultural heritage, and giving up any semblance of earthly security.

North American Mennonitism is itself a significant culture. To embrace it is to move into a socially acceptable sub-group which takes good care of its own. As I called hundreds of unchurched people in Clovis, California, I discovered that Mennonites have a reputation as nice people. Their underlying theology or religious practice tends not to be known, but they are nice people. I have been asked by some, who seemed to have a positive image of Mennonites, whether or not it is a Christian group.

Many of the distinctive beliefs and practices of North American Mennonites trace directly from the Radical Reformation and people like Conrad Grebel. The difference is that these once radical beliefs are now commonplace. The Anabaptists may have invented the separation of church and state, but most people think America's founders originated it.

Those practices for which Anabaptists died are now part of the surrounding culture. A neo-pagan pluralism makes almost any belief system socially acceptable, so long as its adherents are "nice." Where is discipleship in all this?

I believe that we can find the implicit personality theory of Anabaptism in its views on discipleship, but that the same is not necessarily true for modern Mennonites. I also believe that modern Mennonites diverge to some extent from their forebears' personality theory, having adopted modern secular views.

Modern Mennonites often believe, for instance, that people are created good. They agree that people can change, as would any modern personality theorist who hopes to do psychotherapy. If pushed, modern Mennonites would probably agree that we can participate in the divine nature through belief and obedience to God's commands—although they would be vague about what that means.

I see most divergence between modern Mennonites and sixteenth-century Anabaptists in the question of whether personality is truly shown by behavior. Most modern theorists adopt some version of Anderson's "character armor," behind which we are able to hide our true nature.[17]

It is threatening to moderns to think that their inner self can be seen by examining their behavior. That idea is the product of a time and place more in tune with corporate personality, such as medieval Europe. Even so, there continue to be calls from within the Mennonite community for people to act in faithful ways, and thus demonstrate their true character as people of God.

It is here, where behavior and the sense of true inner self converge, that modern questions about discipleship generate most heat. Activists call for a sixteenth-century linkage of the two. Others sound more like Luther. They speak of correct belief and suggest that all are not gifted for "radical discipleship," although they do support those thus called and gifted.

A current example of this phenomenon is the discussion surrounding implementation of Christian Peacemaker Teams. Those Mennonite and Brethren groups which have retained nonresistance as an important tenet of belief are creating a structure outside their denominational institutions for active peacemaking. This will allow more radical discipleship on the part of those called to and gifted for such a life.

While most members of such denominations do not see themselves as participating directly in this work, they want to make it possible for others to do so. In this way they are taking action which demonstrates their inner belief. A sixteenth-century parallel would be Anabaptists who harbored fugitive preachers, although they would not preach themselves. This demonstration of belief, and therefore of underlying personality, is an important part of the CPT idea.

Other groups, for whom the issue of nonresistance has been somewhat more difficult, have chosen to withdraw from CPT. They have cited "concerns about the theological basis for the kinds of activities envisioned for CPT volunteers."[18]

Though respectful of those who feel this way, I believe three things are at work here. First, debate within the group over the propriety of nonresistance as a tenet of belief. Second, disagreement with Anabaptist personality theory which says that inner belief or personality is shown by behavior. Third, acceptance of the Lutheran distinction between public and private behavior.

Those who deny a linkage between inner belief and behavior see an individual's vertical relationship with God as personal and hidden. It is not affected by horizontal relationships demonstrated in outward behaviors, with the exception of gross social impropriety on a personal (though not structural) level. Goodness in personal relationships is seen as a good indicator of the vertical relationship. Avoiding behavior that would put a person at risk with the government is seen as irrelevant.

Sixteenth-century Anabaptists also valued good person-to-person behavior, simply presuming that a Christian would exhibit it. They also valued discipleship that put them in mortal danger. It was not until the eighteenth century that Anabaptists became *die Stillen im Lande*, putting aside behavior that placed one in mortal danger. It is helpful to note that by then, for the most part, Anabaptists had the religious freedom which had been sought by those who risked their lives to witness to their faith.

2. *What lies ahead for modern Mennonites?*

It is interesting that the aspect of Anabaptist personality theory which set it most apart from its neighbors, the belief that personality is shown by behavior, continues to be a problem for modern Mennonites. If we describe beliefs without producing the fruit of that belief, we accommodate to our pluralistic culture, just as medieval Catholics and followers of the magisterial reformers accommodated to theirs. Anabaptists were different in this way. They quoted Jesus:

> Watch out for false prophets. They come to you in sheep's clothing, but inwardly they are ferocious wolves. By their fruit you will recognize them. Do people pick grapes from thornbushes, or figs from thistles? Likewise, every good tree bears good fruit, but a bad tree bears bad fruit. . . . Every tree that does not bear good fruit is cut down and thrown into the fire. Thus, by their fruit you will recognize them (Matt. 7:15-17, 19-20).

I have not given many proof texts to back up the preceding description of Anabaptist beliefs, since the focus of this chapter was to report and analyze rather than to document. However, the transparency of life valued by Anabaptists is described many places by Jesus. It is this scriptural basis which gives power to the Anabaptist understanding.

It is also this basis which makes modern Mennonite discomfort with the linkage of personality and behavior a problem. It wasn't Menno who said "you will recognize the good by their fruit." It was Jesus. This is the consistent witness of Scripture. As we look for ways to follow Jesus without demonstrating that discipleship, we are known by our fruit—or its absence.

To the extent that Anabaptist personality theory as described here diverges from modern Mennonite belief and practice, I believe it is the moderns who skate on thin, unscriptural ice. To be fair, we need to recognize that Mennonites four centuries later are pluralists. The first Anabaptists tore themselves out of their familiar world and separated themselves from friends and family by their radical belief.

Modern Mennonites have tended to see "Mennonite" as an ethnic term. They have placed great value on keeping as many people who are born to Mennonite families "in the fold" as possible. It is a cliché, but also true, that there can be no second generation Mennonite (or Christian, for that matter). Each person must make a personal choice to follow that way.

Violence, Nonviolence, and the Meaning of Nonresistance

As we have seen, contemporary Mennonites tend to be uncomfortable with Anabaptist personality theory and have come to accept the democratic ideal. In twentieth-century North America, this caused Mennonites to develop a special view of the principle of nonresistance.

The effect of the democratic ideal on modern Mennonites is expressed well in this question: "How can you consider disobeying the government when we, the people, are the government?" That view, coupled with the separation of belief and behavior, has sometimes led Mennonites to reject both violent and nonviolent ways of speaking to the existing structures of society.

Nonresistance came to be viewed as a passive thing which permitted leaders to petition government for relief from conscription, for instance. But when anything outside the narrow self-interest of Mennonite pacifists was at stake, it was not acceptable nonresistant behavior to refuse cooperation with the government.

According to our interpretation at least, sixteenth-century Anabaptists followed in the footsteps of Jesus and the apostles by nonviolently confronting sin in societal structures which oppressed the poor. Twentieth-century Mennonites needed to redefine that heritage to square it with their position in American society.

Guy F. Hershberger exemplifies this view in *War, Peace, and Nonresistance*, in the section on nonviolent resistance. After quoting the prophets' condemnation of social injustice, Hershberger says, "It should be noted here, however, that the emphasis in these Scriptures is on *doing justice* rather than on *demanding justice*."

He goes on to note the apostle Paul's instructions to masters for just treatment of slaves. Then he says, "There is no evidence, however, that Paul's quest for justice went beyond a simple statement of his case and an appeal for right."[19] In fairness to Hershberger, he later changed his view on the use of nonviolent direct action in the civil rights struggle.

Mennonites, after obtaining toleration in eighteenth-century Europe, abandoned the prophetic voice for social justice which had led their forebears to risk all for the sake of the gospel. That passivism, along with the seductive power of American democracy and material prosperity, led to renunciation of the nonviolent direct action which brought the free church into being. Nonresistance had been stripped of its power to cause social change, not by persecution, but by prosperity.

This is the nonresistance of which Reinhold Niebuhr wrote when he called Mennonites separationists who had no relevance to the world. He called instead for transformation.

> Nothing is clearer than that a pure religious idealism must issue in a policy of non-resistance which makes no claims to be socially efficacious. It submits to any demands, however unjust, and yields to any claims, however inordinate, rather than assert self-interest against another. . . . This type of moral idealism leads either to asceticism, as in the case of Francis and other Catholic saints, or at least to the complete disavowal of any political responsibility, as in the case of Protestant sects practicing consistent non-resis-

tance, as, for instance, the Anabaptists, Mennonites, Dunkers and Doukhbors.[20]

Had Niebuhr known the dynamic nonresistance of the sixteenth-century Anabaptists, he would have realized that his continuum, to accommodate them, would have to be bent around into a circle. Then transformation and nonresistance would become the dynamic force which so frightened the ruling authorities that they hunted and killed these dangerous people.

Nonresistance, to be faithful to its heritage and to Jesus, must include the possibility of nonviolent direct action challenging rulers in God's name. Jesus, after all, was not killed for his inner belief. He was killed for treasonous behavior which shook the foundations of the state. Inner belief is known only through outward behavior.

A story by Nick Kassebaum of Spokane, Washington, shows how it might be for modern Anabaptists.

> Three, four, five times the train carrying nuclear weapons had gone through Spokane. A local Agape community was the spearhead for demonstrations at each passage of the train.
>
> Agape has a series of watchers throughout the country along the tracks. When news arrives that a train is coming, the community alerts a group of brothers and sisters. They gather to stand beside the tracks with banners and have a news story.
>
> The Spokane community had spent two or three months meeting, planning, and praying together. They kept saying, "Sometime we need to talk about getting up on the tracks, but not this time. We're not ready. We're not together. Sometime we need to say 'no', but not this time. We'll guarantee the police and the railroad that nobody will get up on the tracks. We don't want to be disruptive, we just want to love, to show *agape*."
>
> News of another train came in February 1985. The re-

sponse was the same. I had a real struggle in my soul whether this was the time I personally had to do more than was being said by Agape.

I remember the night before the train came. My wife was out of town, so I was alone. There wasn't the physical embrace, the spoken affirmation, "I know you must do what you must do, and I support you in it."

But late in the evening, I made a couple of telephone calls to persons of the Mennonite community. I simply said, "I think I'm going to be on the tracks tomorrow. I just want you to know that." Those two people chose to go with me, plus another person from the Peace and Justice Center.

The next day, the four of us first met at the Agape prayer circle. We spent about an hour with the rest of the group, going through the ritual in preparation for the train to come—prayers, responsive readings, songs, statements to the press, prepared readings, silence. We were a hundred people, standing in a circle "doing our thing."

I didn't really feel a part of it, because the focus was that we were not yet going to do anything other than pray that the system change. Four of us absented ourselves from the group and went about three blocks down the street. We had our own small preparatory prayer cell.

It was different. We were preparing ourselves not just for passage of the train, but for saying no with our bodies, for breaking the law. We had no idea what the outcome would be—whether we would immediately be arrested or whether the train would not see us. We were giving up control of our lives to give testimony to our hearts.

I recall feeling numb. I tend to be a quiet person in my own spirituality. My praying at that time was for an inner peacefulness that would allow me to be at peace no matter what happened, no matter if it was a legal or even a physical injury. I would not abandon my witness out of fear.

The four of us joined hands. We walked up the embankment to the tracks and sat down together. We were there. We were okay. We began to softly sing one of the songs out of *Sing and Rejoice*.

A helicopter patrolling the tracks saw us and summoned a police van to come. We weren't willing to leave, so the officers had to pick us up and drag us off. They locked us in the van.

They were polite. They knew what we were doing and why. We asked if the van could be turned around so we could watch what went past. They said sure. They turned the van around and got out of the front seat so we would have an unobstructed view of the tracks to watch the train go by. . . .

Death.

Silence.

The train looked like the worst of all that the human community was able to invent. Some of the cars were white, but some had been painted blue, green, pink—Easter egg colors. It was a continued denial of the reality of the train's mission. It was the worst lie I had ever experienced, rolling slowly, slowly, silently down the tracks, taking all of humanity with it.

There we were, locked in a little van, watching this go past. We had said no in a very small way. We learned later that, had we wanted to physically stop the train, if that were more important, we should have picked an isolated area where the police response couldn't have been fast enough.

But we did what we did. It was what I could do at the time in response to nuclear war. I had to say something. I had to *do* something to demonstrate opposition with my body, not just with my words.

My life since then has focused not on opposition techniques, but on creative alternatives. If we can give people real handles to believe in and trust in, we may teach peace more effectively than by only opposing evil.

Victim Offender Reconciliation Program [VORP] is a logical way of expressing this. At VORP, we're actually bringing together victims and offenders, broken human beings. They find healing in each other through a close, personal communication that isn't a part of the criminal justice system. We're demonstrating the positive rather than only demonstrating against the negative.

* * *

At the very beginning of the Anabaptist movement, the yes and the no were in the same act. We challenged the ecclesiastical and political authority who denied the right to believe and do what we felt called to believe and do. "You do not have the right to tell us the basis of our relationship with God. No. We are going to believe otherwise. We are going to act otherwise. Yes."

Suppose we could find ways to both deny the powers of the state and exalt the power of the risen Christ in this way, in the same act. Then we might capture some of the real spiritual power that the early Anabaptist church had to catch the imagination of the world.

So often I talk to people who are disgruntled with the Mennonite Church. They feel we've abandoned the peace position because it gets in the way of evangelism. America and Canada have been too good to us to keep us from looking directly at the evil that allows us to be free. So we look away. We're not bothering anybody. We're not calling into question America's values. We're welcome, as long as we keep paying the bills.

But our experience (in the state of Washington) has been that people come to us because they're looking for someone to offer leadership in peace questions. People look to those from the Mennonite tradition for leadership, guidance, and history for this kind of Christian activity.

At the trial following our trespassing on the tracks, the judge gave us guidelines for designing our own defense. Then he dismissed the case due to a legal error by the prosecution. Partly because of actions such as ours, the "death train" has not been used to transport nuclear weapons for the past two years.

CHAPTER 6
Life Without Violence

Nonresistance Versus Nonviolence

Reinhold Niebuhr had a clear understanding of nonresistance, as shown in the last chapter. Was Niebuhr correct in his assessment of nonresistance as practiced by Mennonites and other followers of the Swiss Brethren?

Niebuhr's basic thesis in *Moral Man and Immoral Society* was that it is a mistake to carry personal Sermon-on-the-Mount morality into the civic arena. He felt this was the mistake Mennonites and their ilk were making. It is certainly true that Mennonites tended not to vote or to accept public office in the United States at the time Niebuhr was writing (original publication was in 1932). Did they also, as he suggests, disavow any political responsibility and accept any unjust demands?

> In the Confederacy, the draft law of 1862 exempted Quakers, Brethren, Nazarenes and Mennonites, with the understanding that they would hire a substitute or pay a tax of $500 to the Confederate treasury. The historic peace churches found these condi-

tions severe and often violated. A number of Mennonites and Brethren were imprisoned and a Church of the Brethren leader in the Shenandoah Valley was shot to death by masked men.[1]

What John Howard Yoder has called "radical subordinationism" was certainly at work in the Mennonite response to such events. The right of the government or vigilantes to require obedience was acknowledged by nonresistant persons. But they accepted the consequences of disobedience rather than violate religious beliefs. "You have the power to kill me, and I will not attempt to kill you to prevent it, but I will not serve in your army or hire a substitute" is how the stance could be summarized.

In some ways, the term *nonresistance* is a misnomer which causes confusion. The attempt to coerce a nonresistant person into actions which violate conscience will be resisted—but not by means likely to produce bodily harm or death to the antagonist.

Niebuhr saw the nonresistant response as passive. It acquiesced in any demand. He equated the pacifist response of not using violent force with passivism. He was mistaken. While nonresistant persons were not willing to use lethal force, they *did* refuse improper demands and used normal lobbying techniques to achieve desired legislation or administrative regulations.

These activities were particularly noticeable in the efforts to obtain conscientious objector status. These efforts are detailed in *The Politics of Conscience*. A key element in obtaining conscientious objector status was the demonstrated willingness of nonresistant persons to go to jail rather than yield to the government's demands for their military service.

It is interesting that Niebuhr sees acceptance of political responsibility in taking elective office but not in going to jail. To obtain legal recognition of the rights of conscientious objectors, nonresistant persons had to commit civil disobedience by refusing to enter the military. What could be more politically responsible?

This acceptance of the consequences of displeasing government authorities goes back to Anabaptist beginnings. Anabaptist believers were willing to accept punishment rather than give in to government demands that violated their understanding of God's will. There is nothing more political than refusing the demands of government authority. What is peculiar about Anabaptists and their modern counterparts is the simple willingness to bear the consequences rather than use violence to prevent the imposition of the government penalty.

A simple declaration of these principles is contained in the minutes of the Brethren in Christ General Conference sessions held June 6-10, 1940.

> . . . and we believe that it teaches nonresistance in a qualified sense, that it is not the Christian's privilege to take up the sword or to fight with carnal weapons; yet it is his duty to be strictly loyal to the government under which he lives in all things that do not conflict with, or are not forbidden by, the Word. . . .[2]

Nonresistance as practiced in America is a doctrine under which lethal violence is rejected as a means of coercion or protection. At the same time, nonresistant Christians prize such nonviolent direct actions as lobbying government officials and refusing to obey government instructions contrary to conscience.

Although some Mennonite groups reject lobbying of officials, no Mennonite groups in America have advocated obeying the government if doing so would require disobeying God. Disagreements about particular nonviolent direct actions have centered on the question of whether obedience to government in a particular case entails disobedience to God.

Lobbying is sometimes done in the halls of Congress

and other times out in the field where government activities take place. Esther Kisamore told the story of her action
with Marge Roberts; it is a story of two women who wanted to lobby against the production of nuclear bombs.

After moving to Colorado, I got involved in some of the
court trials for actions at Rocky Flats. The first weekend a
bunch of us went up to support a woman who had entered
the plant. Momentum was building. Planting a tree seemed
the right thing to do and something I wanted to do. I felt a
sense of urgency.

Marge also wanted to get involved, but she didn't want
to do it alone. I was having that same feeling but didn't
want to jeopardize my work. We agreed to go ahead. We
would take a personal recognizance bond if arrested.

I liked the symbolism at that time of year—close to Palm
Sunday. I was working in the garden at the time and got
the idea of trying to plant a West Virginia dogwood tree at
Rocky Flats because of the story of the dogwood.

According to legend, the blossom is the cross, the crown
of thorns is in the inside, and the drops of blood are on the
petals. The legend has it that the dogwood was once as
sturdy as an oak tree, straight and tall. Being chosen as the
cross of Christ hurt the tree. It asked not to be used again as
a cross. The tree became crippled and the petals became
the shape of the cross and drops of blood and the crown of
thorns.

I had friends of mine send me a dogwood from West
Virginia. The two of us met with friends to plan. The night
before, we met with some of our Mennonite and peace
friends up in Denver. We had a prayer service and potluck
and a fun time with a lot of singing. We stayed with friends
that night.

At five o'clock the next morning, people met with us
and sent us off. Friends followed to see what would happen. We drove into Rocky Flats with the commuter traffic.

It was frightening. My body was shaking. Luckily,
Marge was driving. I'm not sure I would have been able to

drive. I was scared because Rocky Flats is an awesome place, very frightening. The security is heavy. There are so many unknowns. As the resistance community gets stronger, more and more happens. The security people get mad, and you don't know what you're getting into.

We were picked up right at the gate. There had been a series of actions on significant religious days, and they were watching for us. They knew right away we didn't have badges.

They radioed and four or five security cars came driving at us. We got out and said we came to present the tree to them, since obviously we weren't going to get it planted. We had been hoping to plant it close to the plutonium building, where they process the plutonium triggers.

Being handcuffed and shoved into a car produces a helpless and disabling feeling. It is painful to sit in the back of a car without being able to sit against the back of the seat because your hands are cuffed there. It's dehumanizing.

We were trying to make a statement in terms of symbols of things that were life-giving, like a tree. The legend of the dogwood tree itself is a conversion-type message. We had the legend story printed on the card that we left with the dogwood tree for the employees at the plant. We wanted it to make a witness about converting the plant to peaceful uses: "Let's convert Rocky Flats into a place of industry that is life-giving rather than death-giving."

After we were arrested and driven back, we talked to the head of security and asked him to try to keep the tree alive for the trial as an exhibit. It died. I don't know what that says. Evidently the environment there was not conducive to keeping the dogwood alive.

We were taken down to the federal building in Denver and held in a holding tank for a number of hours until arraignment. We were out later that afternoon on a personal recognizance bond.

We pled not guilty and asked for a trial by jury, which we had. We were both found guilty of trespass. Marge was fined $1,000. I was fined $500, with the stipulation that if I didn't get in trouble for two years, I wouldn't have to pay it. But I did get in trouble and they are still trying to collect. I get these threatening letters now and then that say, "We have informed the IRS that you owe us a $500 fine."

I don't pay the fine because I don't want money going back into that system. If I did the action in the first place, I was doing something that was right. I don't feel I owe a fine for going onto "their" land and trying to make a statement of peace, justice, survival, and conversion.

If I knew I was breaking a law, I'd go to jail. That would make a testimony and be a witness. But it would be wrong to pay $500 into a system to which I don't even want to pay taxes.

I had done quite a bit of preparing for this action, trying to make sure close family and friends understood. In a series of tapes, I tried to go through my thoughts and preparation to explain why I had to do this. I played songs which were important to me at the time. I sent the tapes to my past small group, my brothers and mom, and other people close to me.

The whole thing is almost ridiculous, when you think of two middle-aged, simple, common ordinary, women driving into a huge bomb plant—and being considered a threat! That's why you have the fences and extreme security—because the peace community is a threat to them.

We often see ourselves as small and insignificant, yet why do they see us as such a threat? It's humbling and frightening, and a faith kind of thing, to think I'm a threat to them? Look what they have on their side. They have the big guns. They have the police cars with all the armed guards.

But I see it as a strengthening thing. Doing something that simply scares the living daylights out of you, with a friend, builds community. Also important is feeling the protection and care of the community, and the support to do things like that. A sense of being protected by a power greater that myself also comes into play. I feel the strength and protection of God in a situation like that.

How was this action different from lobbying a member of Congress? The plan was to drive in, plant the tree by a building with a card explaining the symbolism of the act, and leave. The action was illegal because the plant was closed to people not there in an official capacity. Let's look at the way one attempt to lobby a member of Congress went.

The things I learned in Bible school and Sunday school have not been wasted, especially the ideas of loving others and a having a nonresistant lifestyle. As we came up through the '60s and '70s, we were aware of Vietnam and were involved in a lot of rallies.

There's a weakness to them. But as it goes along, you realize that this is serious business. Peacemaking is hard work. You try to talk about how you can make this faith that we have *real* in life.

By this time my daughters were getting older. We wanted them to see that Mom and Dad really did try to say "no." So we tried to deal with the government on the tax level. In 1982, we owed them about $500. We decided to say "We're not going to pay it, because we will not pray for peace and pay for war."

The first year we tried this, the FBI garnished our account. People say, "What good did it do? You only witnessed to some IRS agent in Cincinnati. He doesn't care."

We did think about that. But we still felt we had to make a statement, so we did it again the next year. It turns out that most people who hear about it *don't* agree that civil disobedience is an option. The issue is civil disobedience. It threatens people to think about doing something like that.

I was signed up with the Pledge of Resistance, promising to participate in civil disobedience if the United States government backed the *contras* (a guerrilla force opposing the government of Nicaragua). I signed up, thinking I'd never have to do anything about it.

However, our congressman strongly supported the contras. We made several phone calls to talk about our concerns.

One day a number of us went down to his office to meet with him. He wouldn't listen. We decided to stay until he did. I had planned to leave, but the more we talked, the calmer I became. And I felt the need to stay, because the issue was one of my dollars buying destruction. Here I am a Mennonite, a so-called pacifist, paying to kill. So we stayed.

Then the police came. I had an apple. I guess I was the first one out the door, so I ended up on TV eating this apple, with a policeman on one side. I had a smile on my face. It was a good apple.

We got into the paddy wagon and went down to the slammer. Eventually, they let us out. It wasn't a big deal—six or eight hours maybe.

The question is "why?" Why did I do that? I'm not altogether real clear, except that I had to say "no." I took a bus home and all the way I was thinking, What was this all about? But in my heart I was jumping up and down, saying, That's one for us. That's one for the cause.

When I got home my oldest daughter was waiting. She came up and gave me a great, big, old hug and said, "Dad, I'm proud of you." Well, what's important in life? To win some big research award? Or to be daring or stupid enough to say "no?"

We all went down to court and met outside in a big circle, sang songs, and held hands. We talked about how to behave in court—to make clear statements to the judge explaining our actions.

The judge didn't want to hear any statements. He just wanted to get it over with. But we gave our statements anyway. We got fined.

I look back and say, "What good was that?" Well, the good was that, for just for one moment, I tried to put together what I believed and how I acted.

You don't ask "Did it work?" You ask, "Was it worth doing?" It's like being in a play. You have one line. Three sentences or whatever. If you don't do that, then the guy behind you is going to miss his cues. The play won't work right. So it doesn't matter if it's a tiny little "insignificant" thing—you have to do it.

I've become more and more clear that if I'm going to do civil disobedience, it has to be with a group who are doing it because of faith. I don't mind joining hands with all kinds of disciplines, saying "We need to destroy nuclear weapons." But if it comes to civil disobedience, I need to be clear that it's a faith issue, simply because that's where I'm coming from.

I'm *very* concerned about the Mennonite Church. I see Mennonites buying more and more into an ardent combination of patriotism and Christianity. Especially as they become more wealthy, more educated. I don't think we're going to continue to be salty. There are those who are really out in front, key people willing to do the right thing. But the mainstream doesn't want to hear it.[3]

When a member of Congress decides not to see a person asking for an appointment, if that person continues to wait in the office, it becomes illegal trespassing. That is what a "sit-in" is. Waiting to speak to a member of Congress and leaving a tree and card can both become trespassing if that is how the government chooses to define it.

Both are nonviolent direct actions. Both are engaged in by persons who consider themselves followers of the nonresistance advocated by the early Anabaptists. Goals are witnessing to government, making the nonresistant person's beliefs known, and advocating change in government policies.

Is there an element of confrontation in such actions? Certainly. The bomb plant employees did not ask to hear about the women's beliefs. The women simply arrived, forcing the employees to hear them by the nature of the employees' duties.

Does a member of Congress invite conscientious objectors to share their beliefs? Not usually. The lobbying persons appear at the office. Then the nature of the congressperson's job requires that they be dealt with.

When we do anything to make our views known, a form of confrontation is taking place. The exception is when the other person asks about our views first, as sometimes happens to me when I am working on a case for Victim Offender Reconciliation Program.

Nonresistance is not necessarily non-confrontive. When nonresistant people refuse to obey the government, they force the government to deal with them. They demand that the government reckon with their views. It is a call to conversion, unsolicited by the government.

When persons in authority demand things which would violate God's will, a faithful nonresistant person must refuse. That refusal, whatever nonviolent form it takes, is nonviolent direct action. We see no inconsistency between nonresistance as practiced in North America by the spiritual descendants of the Anabaptists and nonviolent direct action. Nonviolent direct action is one way nonresistance works itself out in the world. That is not to say that all nonviolent direct actions are consistent with nonresistance. We turn now to that distinction.

The Anabaptist Heritage of Nonresistance Updated

The *Martyrs Mirror* tells stories of actions consistent with the previous discussion of nonviolent direct action. Anabaptists were ordered by government authorities not to preach and to have their infants baptized. Most run-ins with the authorities related to violations of these requirements.

The other principal area of contention was military service, since Anabaptists refused it during a time of general mobilization. The competing contentions were simple. The authorities required silence and obedient military service. The Anabaptists said either was unfaithful to God—and therefore impossible to perform.

Anabaptists who followed the line of the Swiss Brethren refused to defend themselves with weapons but would try to escape. The classic story is of Dirk Willems, who fled across a frozen canal, only to have his pursuer fall through the ice. Dirk went back and saved the man, who then arrested him. He was executed. Dirk could not be the cause of the man's death, even if it meant his own.

These stories consistently exemplify the refusal of persecuted Anabaptists to use lethal force to protect themselves. They also show the penchant of these people for preaching their views to their persecutors. Life or death was not the issue for these Anabaptists; obedience to God was.

The power of these quiet, pious folks being hunted down, tortured, and killed was great. It led to eventual toleration of their beliefs. It also led to explosive growth for the church in the early years. We want to look further at ways these practices have been the same or different in North America.

Perhaps the greatest difference for North American Mennonites is that they are no longer generally a persecuted minority. When wars and conscription come, there is a time of testing. For the most part, North American Mennonites are quite free to do, say, and believe what they want.

Just as toleration exacted the price of silence in Holland during the seventeenth century, broad toleration of Mennonite views in North America has tended to buy silence. As Mennonites enter the mainstream of society, their economic life is tied to others in the community in new ways.

Tax-exempt status for Mennonite churches and conferences, so long as they do not engage in political activity, has helped the government purchase their silence. Loss of tax-exempt status is perceived by members of churches as a crushing blow. It has been used as an argument against opposing government policies.[4]

Since Mennonites are usually not on the run in contemporary North America, they have no automatic call to express their beliefs. If you are suddenly arrested for being an Anabaptist, you have the opportunity to express your beliefs to your persecutors. If you are arrested for refusing to register for the draft or refusing to pay taxes, you have an opportunity to express your motivation to those processing you.

Few Mennonites find themselves in either position these days. The issues have changed. We are ruled by a democratically elected government and have significant opportunities to lobby the government in ways acceptable to it. For the most part, Mennonite religious practices are of no interest to the government.

Mennonites today experience a government which will leave us alone if we leave it alone and pay our taxes. Normal Mennonite behavior is perfectly acceptable to society. Persecution takes place all around us, but tends not to be persecution of Mennonites as a group. This is a change from the sixteenth- and seventeenth-century experiences which shaped the face of Anabaptism. Rather than being the persecuted minority, Mennonites in North America are often part of the persecuting majority, whether or not they are aware of it.

Take any issue—treatment of prisoners, the developmentally disabled, the mentally ill, Native Americans, African Americans, the poor, those living in other countries under United States supported dictatorships or third-world debt. In relation to such issues, most Mennonites belong to the group in power, not the powerless group.

This is a significant historical change. Even though Mennonites still tend not to hold elective office, they play important roles in the social and economic life of their communities. Thus instead of being persecuted, Mennonites find themselves implicated in the persecution of others. When they care for the powerless, they are feeling concern for people other than themselves.

This change means that the actions of Mennonites engaged in nonviolent direct action have no apparent direct bearing on their own lives. Such acts can look like meddling or activism for its own sake. Mennonites begin to look like troublemakers when they try to help. People may feel deeply implicated in the government's unjust treatment of Salvadoran refugees, for instance. Yet many will still consider them "outside agitators."

Challenging Worldly Power

What it comes down to is this: Is it proper for a nonresistant person to directly and nonviolently oppose worldly power which makes demands contrary to the gospel?

Carol Rose, the teller of the following story, is a Mennonite who grew up in a Presbyterian family. After college she worked with refugees in Texas under Mennonite Voluntary Service. Then she joined Mennonite Central Committee for a three-year term in Honduras. As part of her assignment in Honduras, Carol worked with a United Nations presence at the Honduras/El Salvador border. This was necessary because the Honduran military had a record of killing refugees who arrived without international accompaniment.

> We get up at the break of dawn. Roosters are crowing. The United Nations officials and I roll up our cots. We put on our shoes and make sure we have our passports and water. One of the officials tells the army we're going out to the border.
> It's just starting to get light. We walk over cobblestones and past adobe houses. Toward the edge of town, there are

more shacks with grass thatch roofs. Then we walk down into a creek and up the other side. It's quite a walk—three or four kilometers as the crow flies.

It's a lovely hike. Honduras is beautiful. It's the beginning of the dry season, so it's starker than at other times. In some seasons there are flowers everywhere. The creek is still flowing, so we have to take our shoes off, cross, then put the shoes back on. In the shade there are still green grasses and flowers. In my Bible I have pressed one of the flowers from this particular day. It was bright yellow; it's now faded brown.

We arrive at one of the "understood" meeting places just this side of the Salvadoran border. There is no direct communication. We go by word-of-mouth as to whether there are refugees coming, or we just walk out to the places we know we will find them.

Then we wait. We know that if there is a group ready to come, somebody on the Salvadoran side will see us and get the refugees. There are always mosquitoes and insects flying around. They bite you; the bites get infected.

This day we wait in an area where there used to be a village. During the turbulent years when the refugees first fled into Honduras, that village was ransacked and some of the people were killed by the Salvadoran or Honduran military. The rest of the residents fled. People from the next village down still plant corn fields there. They even plant inside the ruined, roofless homes.

I have brought along a few scraps of paper; I sit and write poetry and letters. Given the likelihood of seeing the military in the near future, I don't write anything the least bit political—although it's hard for me to write poetry that's not!

It's a beautiful land. I figure a good way to pass time in praise, as well as to let people know we're here, is to sing, and so I do. Then—.

"Oh, they're here!" A surprise. A breaking in on ordinary time. It reminds me of *kairos*, one of the words for time in Greek. It's not ordinary time. It breaks in and goes beyond.

There are two families. This day is unusual because one family is whole—father, mother, and children. Usually families are like the other family in this group in which the father has died. They're all tired. They have been walking for days.

It's so amazing and humbling to have these Salvadoran families looking at us. The relief on their faces says, Oh! No military. People that want to meet us and walk with us, and make sure we're safe.

To be invited into that moment, when a person is fleeing from war and loss of life, is like being present at a birth or a death. It's a great privilege to walk with people in that sacred moment.

The father is carrying a two-year-old daughter on his shoulders. The mother holds a one-year-old on her hip. Then there's the other mother with two children. One probably six. She's carrying a toddler on her hip. They don't have anything except the clothes on their backs.

The man has molded plastic shoes, like the cheapest rubber boots you could think of buying in the States. But they're hard plastic, not rubber—cracked and tied together with string. They must be tremendously uncomfortable. The women are both barefoot, as are all of the kids.

You have to imagine, these people have been walking for days over hard trails, through brush, over rock. One of the women has fairly bad infections on her legs, because she hasn't had access to clean water.

We don't talk a lot. There is already so much trust implied in just their showing up that I never ask questions. The people are already risking so much and need to feel that we accept them as they are. They don't have to prove to me that they're refugees. We can hear the bombs from this side of the border.

As we walk down and through a couple of villages, the toddler on the father's shoulders sees something and says, "*Mira!* Look, Look! It's a goat, it's a goat! A chicken, a chicken! A rooster, rooster, rooster!"

Our trip down is full of this litany of everything she

sees. The transition from fear to trust that they'll make it comes through in the children as well their parents.

We go down the hill over the same rocks and creeks, up and down and around the hills, stopping to rest more frequently because there isn't any hurry. Contact made, the time is ours—time to enjoy the child's comments, the flowers by the roadside, or the trail.

Going into the town, we go straight to the house rented by the United Nations. A United Nations person goes to the military command post and tells them they need to register some new refugees. The military comes and asks questions. They have forms to fill out. In the meantime, I cook up some *arroz con leche* (rice and milk). They've eaten only green mangoes for days.

I stay close enough to make sure the military doesn't intimidate the people, although just the soldiers' presence is threat enough. My presence is to counterbalance theirs, except that I don't have a United States–provided M-16 machine gun.

After the military has the information they need, we all fit into the back of a pickup. They send a military foot-soldier with us "to protect the refugees."

"Who are you protecting them from?" I ask.

I am there to protect the Salvadoran refugees from the Honduran military. Who the military thinks they are protecting the refugees from, I really don't know.

After a long ride we get to the town of San Marcos and check in. We present a copy of the military's acknowledgment of these refugees to the immigration officials. They go through the whole process again. Another tense and threatening time. Then we go up to the Mesa Grande refugee camp just outside of town. There we go through the military checkpoint and through the whole list one more time.

Finally we get to go into the refugee camp. The Salvadorans already in refuge there prepare dinner for them—a joyous reception. There are several hundred people around to look anxiously for family members.

The coordinators (Salvadorans) of the camp ask them, "Where are you from? Who are your family members?"

When assigned a place to live, they will be with family if at all possible, which in this case *is* possible. Cousins and aunts shuffle around a little to make extra space for them.

By that time it is night. I go looking for a cold shower and a cot and go to bed.

* * *

I became a member of the Mennonite Church in Honduras. I think the Honduran Mennonites are very learned about what it is to be a Mennonite.

"When people are in need," they say, "you are required to respond as a Christian."

That is central to my understanding of the gospel. And I think it's key to an Anabaptist understanding of the gospel. I was sent to the border area to focus on the needs of the refugees and to stand by them. When I heard that there were refugees at the border, I didn't have an option not to go; they were neighbors in need.

Christ was clear that faithfulness entails risk. In many ways it's harder to work that out in North America than in Central America, because the risks in Central America are obvious.

While preaching in church in Malpulaca, I've had soldiers with their M-16 machine guns show up in the doorway, listening. You know it's a risk to continue with a faithful interpretation of some Scriptures in that situation. But what option do you have? An unfaithful interpretation of the Scripture is not an option.

Living in the border area and dealing with the military also challenged my view of enemies. Before going down, I always thought, Love your enemies? I must be really good at it, because I can't think of anybody I consider an enemy.

Now I don't think that commandment has to do with not having enemies. I think Jesus knew who his adversaries were. In Honduras, the enemies were the ones who wanted to harm the people I wanted safe.

I was called to love these people? It's not something I fully learned. I did learn to treat them nicely so they wouldn't hurt me or the people I was trying to protect, but that's not what love means.

Unlike the United Nations officials, I was there on behalf of the church, on behalf of God. When the Honduran military was doing something wrong, I didn't need to think about my subordinate position to the government, only about my position in relation to God and the people.

So at what point does love require that I challenge these authorities? At what point does love require that I call them to conversion? Would I not be risking my own security, the security of the Honduran Mennonites, and the security of the refugees? There's no one answer to these questions. One must discern when to speak and when to let simple presence sing the challenge.[5]

Carol's presence was not desired by the Honduran government. She was an outside agitator interfering in the internal affairs of a sovereign state. Her mere presence was a challenge to the army. Was her ministry of presence nonviolent direct action? Yes. Was it nonresistant? What could be more consistent with the Swiss Brethren and all their progeny?

Let us move back to Chicago for a comparison. During the 1987 Christmas season, twelve persons, including Gene Stoltzfus of Chicago (the storyteller here), entered Water Tower Place in Chicago. Their purpose, there in one of the Midwest's best known and most elite shopping centers, was to sing Christmas carols honoring the memory of people in Central America.

Three days prior to this action, Water Tower Place requested a court order prohibiting people from entering to sing or pass out leaflets. Despite the ensuing court order, the twelve entered and were arrested while singing Christmas carols. They were charged with criminal trespass. By engaging in that protest, they also violated the court order and were therefore in contempt of court.

Two days later, on December 23, the group again entered Water Tower Place. They sang after delivering letters to the security people and the merchants of Water Tower place explaining their act. Again the court issued an order prohibiting the protest. Eight participants were arrested for criminal trespass.

In the subsequent trial, twelve of the group were found guilty and sentenced to one to six months of supervision by the probation department. What follows is Gene's statement before the court on June 7, just before sentencing.

> Your Honor, I am 47 years old and have spent about half of my adult life working and traveling in more than thirty countries around the world. I have clear and strong feelings about the people with whom I have worked. They are struggling for an economic chance.
>
> In my international work, I have been in hundreds, perhaps thousands, of marketplaces around the world. The marketplace reaches more than 4,000 years into history and is an institution established to exchange goods, services, and ideas. Your Honor, only in this country have I been arrested for exchanging ideas in the marketplace.
>
> When I went to Water Tower Place to sing, I carried with me my colleagues and companions from around the world. And in this season of peace, I chose to remember them.
>
> Your Honor, I am an eighth-generation American. My first American ancestor came here in 1764. I can look back through seven generations of Mennonite ministers who have lived in this land. My foreparents came here in order to gain religious freedom and economic opportunity. They came for the same reasons that people are struggling in places like Central America.
>
> They also came to escape persecution. Many had died

or been tortured because of their convictions. I am proud to spring from these roots. America has been very good to me. But when I measure its kindness to me against its treatment of my friends in other lands, my pride turns to ambivalence.

Your Honor, in human history and particularly in my own history, the marketplace has been, not only a place of exchange of goods and ideas, but also the site where punishment is carried out. If you choose to punish me, Your Honor, I would invite you to consider having me manacled and placed in the mezzanine of Water Tower Place for a period of not less than one month.

There is something about "political demonstrations" which Mennonites have seen as worldly, having nothing to do with nonresistance. The original Anabaptists did not engage in the same kind of demonstrations for the simple reason that their living of transformed lives was illegal in itself.

The same type of living is perfectly legal today in North America. So we find no natural outlets for witnessing to our faith. What continues to skirt the edges of legality is calling for systemic change. It is the difference between running an ambulance service at the foot of a dangerous mountain road and lobbying the highway department to make the road safer.

But are things now so different from the sixteenth century? The original Anabaptists were not calling for toleration of their individual beliefs. They were calling for transformation of the religious and governmental structures of their day. They engaged in public disputations, cried out their belief as they were being executed, and made a lot of noise trying to cause change.

Some Anabaptists did settle for toleration, but many continued to push for societal transformation until it cost them their lives. *That* is nonresistance. To make a prophetic call for change, to lay your life on the line, and to accept the consequences rather than to protect yourself by force, is the basis of nonresistance.

David Hayden, a pastor and a director of Justice House in Roanoke, Virginia, tells of a nonviolent direct action project originating out of a community of fifty homeless people.

As a pastor and Pledge of Resistance organizer in Ashville, North Carolina, Hayden had observed the effect of tourist development on the poor. In Roanoke, Hayden combined creative nonviolence with homelessness advocacy, witnessing against a proposal by the city to build a $359-million tourist complex.

Hayden explains how this project grew out of an atmosphere of Christian community of the poor, Bible study, group meetings, and theological groundwork within the Anabaptist/Mennonite tradition.

> Soon after our coming to Roanoke and establishing Justice House, the Explore project burst on the scene. Proposed were a zoo, theme park, and tourist development.
>
> Homelessness was not an issue at that point. "There are no homeless people in Roanoke," said the authorities.
>
> We started to work against the Explore project. We spoke at a public rally. We became visible. One TV station picked it up. It organized a five-day series on homelessness around Justice House.
>
> The response from the establishment was typical: "Well, they're just agitators, stirring up trouble."
>
> But after that series, the TV station people called and said they had never experienced anything like it. They were swamped with phone calls. Folks were aghast that homelessness was a problem in their city. That was the pivotal point.
>
> After the Explore promoters had designed the project and done political lobbying, they said, "Now we're going

to ask the public what they think and where we should put the elephant pen."

You can easily understand how we would look at a project that proposed to build a zoo to house animals—when we were homeless. We started talking about it and got spontaneous responses from members of the community. So we made our presence known at the Explore public meetings, handing out flyers and so forth.

The laugh-box disruption was the result of things just not working in these meetings. Actually, I think the laugh box idea began through divine inspiration. I woke up in the middle of the night, saying, "Laugh boxes!" I didn't even know there were such things. Remember, this is Virginia. Civility is required. So we went and purchased a bunch of laugh boxes.

An Explore meeting had been called where they had the county planners and political folks on their side. They arranged the meeting through them—it gave Explore a sense of legitimacy. They did a slick, well-orchestrated presentation. I liken it to the old traveling, snake-oil salesman. The snake oil wasn't all it was cracked up to be, and neither was this project. It would drive property values up and increase homelessness. We were trying to bring attention to that.

Fifteen folks from Justice House went to the meeting. We sat down very nicely. We had four laugh boxes. We had planned to wait until they got to the presentation of what a great economic benefit this was going to be.

The Explore representative got up to the podium. Our laugh boxes went off. There was absolute silence. Now they knew why we were here, this nonviolent Mennonite pastor and 15 homeless people.

We sat there, very polite. Pretty soon people got enough nerve to turn around and look. Somebody snickered. The guy stopped talking. There was quite a hubbub. Pretty soon some people were shouting and getting angry.

I stood and quoted Mary's Magnificat, "He has brought down rulers from their thrones . . ." (Luke 1:46-55).

* * *

We had made our point, because under the guise of free speech, we don't have free speech. In the name of truth, they speak untruth.

After it happened, Ed Loring wrote me, "The laughter is great. God laughs at the plans of mice and men."

The laughter symbolized the absurdity of what they were saying in a way that was nonviolent. That was the reason for it.

We're a base community, not in theory, but in practice. Base communities are communities of poor people. I believe the poor are a channel of God's revelation. Churches of the poor are the model for Christ's church.

It's interesting that when you become identified with the poor, the gluttons, the drunkards, as we are in this community, you experience the same opposition Jesus did. Rejection comes if you really enter the world of the poor and from that context say "yes" to the kingdom of God and "no" to what is anti-kingdom.

I think that's what makes identifying with the poor difficult. It's painful. There's no question about that. It's awfully painful. Justice, or peacemaking, as we say, is a messy business.

Is it nonresistant to disrupt a public relations show for a zoo which will displace poor people? Is something that makes people in power angry Christlike? The laugh box routine has much in common with Jesus' cleansing of the temple. Jesus so angered the people in power that "the chief priests and the teachers of the law heard this and began looking for a way to kill him, for they feared him, because the whole crowd was amazed at his teaching" (Mark 11:18).

When we enter the place of worldly power and confront it with the truth, we are following in Jesus' steps. The response we get is the same response he got. Nonresistance is so powerful it can inspire murderous rage from those it confronts. The call to conversion is only welcomed by those few who have been prepared by God to receive it gladly. As Jesus says, "No one can come to me unless drawn by the Father who sent me; and I will raise that person up on the last day" (John 6:44, NRSV).

When we are faithful to the nonresistance of Jesus, anger and hatred follow. The idea that we must be liked by other people to be faithful does not come from Jesus. Justice for the poor and oppressed come at the expense of those in positions of power. They will always oppose such efforts.

Nonresistance confronts injustice nonviolently, but resolutely. Doing this generates energy which makes change possible. So long as the status quo is unchallenged, there is no energy for change. We become collaborators in the injustice which exists. To become a collaborator with injustice is to deny the gospel.

> The Spirit of the Lord is on me, because he has anointed me to preach good news to the poor. He has sent me to proclaim freedom for the prisoners and recovery of sight for the blind, to release the oppressed, to proclaim the year of the Lord's favor. (Luke 4:18-19)

CHAPTER 7
Rediscovering Nonresistance

March 12, 1989[1]

Fresno Police arrested 120 chanting anti-abortion demonstrators Saturday who violated a court order and blocked the entrance to a downtown family planning clinic.

Operation Rescue demonstrators began to gather at the Family Planning Associates at 165 N. Clark St. shortly before 7 a.m. After three hours, protesters who volunteered to be arrested sat down and went limp after police ordered the crowd to disperse.

A few children wept as the demonstrators were carried by police to waiting city buses. Onlookers shouted, "Don't hurt them."[2]

September 22, 1989

A Fresno Municipal Court judge denied Thursday a prosecutor's request to restrict attorneys from publicly commenting on the misdemeanor trespassing trial of six abortion protesters. . . .

"I'm just trying to limit the amount of coverage," [the prosecutor] said.

For three days the defense attorney has been previewing the "necessity defense" he wants [the judge] to allow in the presence of the jury. He claims the protesters broke the law by trespassing at Family Planning Association out of necessity. They sought to stop "a greater evil"—abortions—he said.[3]

November 3, 1989

The defense attorney in the Fresno Municipal Court trial of seven anti-abortionists faces a contempt-of-court jail term as soon as the trial ends.

[Judge] stopped the misdemeanor trespass trial twice Thursday to add five days onto a two-day sentence he gave the defense attorney after the jury was selected last week.

"I'm going to serve the time," he vowed. "I can't be a silent conspirator in the crime against humanity."

[The attorney] said he would defy the judge's orders not to attempt to prejudice or indoctrinate the jury about abortion. . . .

In contempt hearings after [the judge] had sent the jury out of the courtroom, the attorney told the judge that during the Nuremburg war crimes trials after World War II, judges were convicted for their roles in the Holocaust. "The abortion holocaust far surpasses the Nazi Holocaust in the number of human beings killed."[4]

November 9, 1989

A divided jury, unable to unanimously conclude that seven protesters had trespassed at a Fresno abortion clinic, closed the curtains Wednesday on the latest installment of the [defense attorney] show.

[The judge] declared a mistrial after the jurors, split 10-2 for conviction, said it did not appear likely that they could ever reach agreement. . . .

In a September trial of six abortion protesters in Fresno Municipal Court, a jury spent less than half an hour deciding that the defendants were guilty of trespassing, unlawful assembly, and failing to disperse. . . .

If the mistrial can be defined as a success for [the defense attorney], its price could be very high. [The judge] rained down contempt orders upon [the attorney] for his repeated violations of the judge's order not to ask inflammatory questions.

[The attorney's] rhetoric, however, is what the case is all about. He seeks to use the courts as a forum for the anti-abortion movement. He wants jurors, before they can decide whether his clients are guilty of trespassing, to consider whether they are answering to a higher law.[5]

March 3, 1990

All but 20 of 136 anti-abortion rights protesters awaiting trials in Fresno Municipal Court pleaded no contest Friday to refusing to leave doorways of a Fresno abortion clinic when ordered away by police last year.

[The judge] also allowed the 116 Operation Rescue followers who chose to accept conditional sentences of one year to remain free.

The conditions of that freedom are that they obey laws and pay a $100 fine.

"I feel that we've done what's right for the people of the county," [the prosecutor] said. "We're attempting to stay with our position that you can't violate the law, but you can still make your feelings known."[6]

Nonviolent direct action used to be the exclusive province of people usually referred to as "the left." We expected protests and marches to be led by peace groups, or civil rights groups.

That convenient distinction no longer exists. Nonviolent direct action has found a friend in conservative religious groups in the United States. They feel called by God to work against things they see as unhealthy permissiveness, moral decay, or worse.

In Operation Rescue's view, the stakes are high: preventing the murder of millions of people. If that is how you see legal abortion, blockading clinic doors seems a trifling response in comparison to the evil being confronted. People who believe the building of nuclear weapons is a crime against humanity and sin against God are in the same position.

If you are satisfied that faithfulness to God and silence in the face of monstrous destruction of human life are incompatible, what do you do?

The sixteenth-century Anabaptists were faced with such

a situation, both in the war against the Turks, and in the persecution of their own movement. They responded to the universal conscription of their day by refusing to join the army, even when such refusal meant death.

They also refused to participate in the system of government which prosecuted the war and persecution. Not only did they refuse to participate, they preached boldly against the killing and defended themselves in court or in public disputations.

It took many years for the initial fires of Anabaptism to become acceptance of the right to exist in exchange for silence. That heritage of silence continues to affect the heirs of those Anabaptists. In North America, Mennonites tended to speak up only when their own particular interests were attacked, as in the case of conscription.

However, when the American civil rights movement adopted practices akin to those of sixteenth-century Anabaptists, some Mennonites did wake up to their past and used nonviolent direct action. As the vineyards of America provided new plantings when the blight killed off the vineyards of France, so the civil rights movement reawakened Mennonites to their own heritage.

Here and there pockets of people began to study Anabaptist history. They sensed God calling them to action beyond what two centuries of quietness had taught. They rediscovered not the "Anabaptist vision" of Harold S. Bender, but the vision of Blaurock, Grebel, and Manz, who defied their government and their church in God's name.

It's happening again. Others are discovering this heritage and holding it up for us to see. As Charles Scriven writes, "The Anabaptists are back. Though maligned and dismissed for centuries, these Reformation radicals are today winning the admiration of many theologians."[7]

What is winning this admiration? The discovery that the Anabaptists believed in doing what Jesus said, not just believing it in their heads. What a needed idea, that being a disciple means doing the radical things Jesus said to do.

As Scriven goes on to say, "[For Anabaptist writers] Christ is the last word. And the suggestion is that recognizing this means defying much of conventional Christian wisdom, including the commonplace dismissal of New Testament nonviolence."[8]

A reading of sixteenth-century Anabaptism which describes their nonresistance in the beginning as passive is incorrect. A reading of subsequent Mennonite history which describes their nonresistance as passive is much nearer the truth. Mennonites have, for the last two hundred years, been selective in their memory of the Anabaptist heritage, remembering the activism of the movement only when conscription threatened.

What is happening today among Mennonites is a rediscovery of the original Anabaptist vision in which nonresistance was a dynamic force for social transformation. The question for us is not so much, Which is correct? as, Which is faithful to Jesus Christ? This book has argued that the use of nonviolent direct action to achieve social transformation is both the best modern expression of the belief of sixteenth-century Anabaptism—and the way to faithfulness.

We turn to Central America for a story. John Paul Lederach, a Mennonite Central Committee worker, found himself mediating between the Sandinista government of Nicaragua and the Miskito Indians.

> When you begin to work between a resistance group that has chosen armed struggle and a government that has been fighting a war for the last eight years, how do you sort out what is truth and what is not?
>
> Because of my role as mediator between the Miskito Indians and the Sandinistas, I have been chased around by the Costa Rican police, the CIA, and the contras [United

States-backed counter-revolutionaries]. They have threatened to kidnap my daughter and assassinate me. In March, I experienced yet another angle on understanding truth in this kind of complex situation.

We had decided that the exiled Indian leaders would take a two-week trip throughout the East Coast of Nicaragua, visiting villages to talk about the progress that had been made in our negotiations.

The government in Managua agreed. During the last five or six days, there was to be a public meeting in Puerto Cabezas. Brooklyn Rivera, the main Indian leader, was to address the largest crowd of the whole trip.

On Saturday, the day before the actual meeting, thirty people, a mob, arrived at the hotel where my delegation was staying. They ransacked the hotel, throwing rocks, tearing out windows, and creating quite a scene. Police and military people came and watched. They did nothing to stop the violence or control the crowd. We were eventually able to control the damage by happening to arrive at the right time.

Local officials claimed the reason for this mob activity was the Indian leadership "calling people back to war." This was not the case. The officials said they had "little control over the mobs themselves," which again was not the case.

The position of the Indian leadership was very clear. They would not back down. They would proceed with the public meeting. The position of the mediation team was very clear. The only protection the Indians had was if we were with them. If we were positioned in and among them, there would be less likelihood of violence than if they went on their own.

I remember clearly the Sunday we as a conciliation commission (three from the Moravian Church, myself a Mennonite, and Dr. Parajon of the Baptist Church), met to discuss how we were going to approach the day. We had a time of prayer, which was the most powerful prayer I have ever been involved in. We talked not only about ourselves and our fears, but about the people who we knew were going to do violence against the crowd. We left the house knowing we probably would return with physical injuries.

The meeting involved a long march to the baseball stadium by about 1,500 Indians. At two o'clock, a mob of about seventy began to appear. They came armed with bricks, chains, and clubs.

Directly behind the stadium is the office of the Ministry of the Interior, with machine guns and anti-aircraft equipment lined up in front of it. Suddenly everything went off—machine guns, anti-air cannons, and mortar cannons. They claimed there were planes flying over, boats approaching, and troops coming in.

All of this was fabricated to create a lot of confusion. Brooklyn's speech obviously was not heard by anybody, but was given out of principle more than anything else. The mobs were located back in the stadium, shouting back and forth with the crowd.

At the end of the speech, Brooklyn Rivera came down off the back end of a pickup truck where he was standing. A government official said, "Get Dr. Parajon and Brooklyn into the pickup and drive them out before something happens."

Brooklyn said very clearly, "No, I'm going to walk home."

Dr. Parajon, about fifty or sixty years old, walking with a limp and wearing a baseball cap, said, "Well, I'm going with Brooklyn."

So you had five or six hundred Indians, with Brooklyn and Parajon in the middle, walking out of the stadium. All along the periphery of this big crowd, violence erupted. Rocks. Bricks. The Indians responded with the same kind of violence. They had obviously never been prepared nor were willing to act in a nonviolent manner.

It was a typical riot scene. A group of about twenty or thirty of the mob came running back into the stadium and began attacking a fifty-year-old man. One of the Moravian pastors on our commission was attempting to stop the behavior.

Suddenly the shout went out, "There's the North American, let's get him!" They came running toward us. A rock hit me. We jumped on the truck and locked the doors. The first thing that hit the truck was a chain that shattered the windshield. Glass splattered all over my face and arms. The guy beside me drove out through the gate. Somehow, we didn't hit anybody.

All the windows were smashed. I was hit in the back of the head with rocks. A two-by-four was brought down on my shoulder. The driver was clubbed with a boulder and needed seven stitches in the back of his head. Still he drove a block and a half through about forty more of these people just waiting for us with bricks and rocks. Certainly if the mob had stopped us, they would have killed us.

Finally we reached the crowd of Miskitoes. They opened up, then shut back down with the truck in the middle. We were taken to the hospital, where I was stitched up by a Cuban doctor. Somehow we had gotten out of there alive.

When we got back to Managua, both sides, actually in quite a mature manner, said this kind of an incident helped clarify where the real reconciliation needed to take place. Interior Minister Borge promised to travel personally with the Indians to the East Coast to help rechannel and rebuild dialogue where conflict was taking place.

Then you come to this awful question of what truth is. Whom do you believe? If you take just that incident, I could say, "This is how the Sandinistas behave. They don't know how to negotiate—they only deal with sticks and bricks and guns." That is not the experience we had at the national level. But that certainly was the experience I had that day.

Central America is not a place where you're going to find some guys in white hats and some guys in black hats. That is what our government and the mass media tend to do. They try to create an image of who is and who is not right or wrong. What I have found is that, on all sides, there can be complexity and diversity.

Was John Paul Lederach practicing nonresistance when he accompanied the Indian leader? Yes. Was John Paul practicing nonresistance when he put himself in such a position in the first place? That is the question over which Mennonites have tended to disagree. Social transformation cannot come about without putting oneself in such positions, but to do so is far from being passive.

The vision of Christian Peacemaker Teams is to place people where conflict makes social transformation possible through creative nonviolent direct action. To put oneself in harm's way as a witness to Jesus' way of nonresistance is to be salt and light in the world.

Kathy Royer wrote this account of her experience in the first "Faith and Resistance Retreat" in 1985, while she was on the staff of MCC U.S. Peace Section.

> The window just to my right reflected the faces of those who were gathered in the large sanctuary of the Holy Rosary Catholic Church in Glenwood, Iowa. They had gathered to think and pray about the sinful use of nuclear weapons. Their reflections were superimposed on a group of local church members gathered behind that window in a small prayer chapel to pray for peace.
>
> I was part of the large group of approximately 500 who had come together from all over the United States. We were diverse. Some of us were active in social justice concerns in the communities in which we lived. We were a vital group. We were action-oriented. We sang, prayed, and discussed.
>
> We were passionate and serious and boisterous as we pondered the possibility of moving outside the law. We wanted to communicate our concern about the proliferation of machines of death and destruction to those in power at the Strategic Air Command just twenty miles away.
>
> We were together for two days, from early morning until late at night. All the while, the silent prayer vigil continued in the small chapel. We could see young men and

women—some obviously teenagers—come and go. We watched during the day as older people—possibly retired—knelt with worn rosaries in their hands.

Sometimes working men would come and kneel, still dressed in their khaki work clothes. Other times there were young mothers. I didn't talk to the people who were praying, but their presence gave me an energy and a power I had not experienced before.

I came to the retreat from a life that had taught me that Jesus is the answer. My parents' strong faith taught me that Christianity makes a difference in every part of life. As I grew, I became aware that sin was rampant in the world. I saw with my own eyes the raw violence of life in southern Africa. I came to the conclusion that if Jesus is the answer, then he must be in the midst of the terrible sin of the world.

I understood from what I had learned about Jesus that his followers were responsible to be his messengers in the world. To me the message became clear. If Jesus is the answer, then I am called to be the messenger. This was a frightening conclusion. I was scared when I went to Iowa.

As I sat in that church for those two days, I thought of many reasons why I could not or should not take Jesus' message to the people making and planning war at the Strategic Air Command. I thought of my two children back in Indiana—what jeopardy would they be in if I risked carrying Jesus' message? I thought about the likely futility of my act.

Now and then, as I pondered these questions, I glanced through the window at my right. I would see those people praying for peace. I would feel the power of the prayers and I knew I was part of that prayer.

They were doing their part. Could I do mine? As my face was reflecting on the glass through which I could see the people in prayer, so were we connected to one another—those praying and I.

I felt the strength of their silent vigil. I knew I could offer myself to be at least part of the way in which their prayers could be embodied in action. I knew that their prayers would be empty without real, flesh-and-blood people to carry the message of Jesus to the world. I also knew that, without the power of the Spirit of God, my action would be weak.

On the last night of the retreat, I decided. I would go with those who were going to speak to the generals. I knew that I would be breaking the law, because the generals did not want to talk with us. I also knew that I was empowered by my prayers and the prayers of those around me. I knew that the message of the gospel needed to be carried into the midst of the sinful world. I was ready.

The next morning, as we met for worship, we could still see the people gathered to pray in the small chapel. My eyes moved from the crucifix that hung before us to my reflection in the chapel window, then beyond to the people kneeling in prayer. I joined my voice with those around me as we sang a song which summed up my feelings: "Here I am Lord, is it I Lord? I have heard you calling in the night. I will go, Lord, if you lead me. I will hold your people in my heart."[9]

One thing all these stories have in common might lead us astray. That is what Stanley Hauerwas and William Willimon have styled "heroic individualism."[10] Anabaptists had their heroes, and we moderns do too. The danger is that we will treat the individual actions of heroes as the goal. Only as Anabaptists formed themselves into the church, the body of Christ, did their individual heroism have its meaning. From within the church comes discipleship. From outside the church comes heroic individualism.

Kathy Royer does not write of her personal heroism, but of the power she discovered in the gathered body. Blaurock, Grebel, and Manz did not baptize themselves; they baptized one another.

In the same way, the goal of Christian Peacemaker Teams is not to facilitate individual action. It is to create a community of disciples who will, together, live faithful lives. They are to become communities grounded in Christ and modeling his nonresistant, transforming life to the world, to his glory.

Ronald J. Sider describes the creation of Christian Peacemaker Teams this way.

> In December 1986 the Mennonite and Brethren in Christ Churches of North America completed an extensive two-year exploration of a proposal to establish peacemaking teams trained to intervene in situations of violent conflict using the techniques of King and Gandhi. Abandoning the category of "nonresistance" as the dominant definition of their pacifism, they called for "caring, direct challenge of evil." And they endorsed the establishment, training, and deployment of Christian Peacemaker Teams using non-violent direct action.[11]

Sider's interpretation is certainly legitimate. One could also, however, interpret what happened as a redefinition of nonresistance. I think those present recognized that "caring, direct challenge of evil" was part of faithful nonre-sistance.

Discipleship is a journey, a following of Christ through-out life. As the world awakens to the power of nonviolent direct action shown by Jesus, the historic peace churches also recognize it as a valid part of their witness. As they do, they move from loving peace to making peace in a danger-ous world.

Notes

Preface
1. *The Lectionary for the Christian People, Cycle C.* (New York: Pueblo Publishing Co., 1988), p. 250.

Chapter 1
1. See, for example, the extended discussion of types and levels of violence in Duane K. Friesen, *Christian Peacemaking and International Conflict* (Scottdale, Pa.: Herald Press, 1986), pp. 143 ff.
2. Confront—1. to face, especially in challenge: oppose; 2. a: to cause to meet: bring face-to-face b: to meet face-to-face: encounter. *Webster's Ninth New Collegiate Dictionary*, (1983). David Augsburger gives a particularly helpful definition in *Caring Enough to Confront* (Scottdale, Pa.: Herald Press, 1973), p. 53: "Confrontation invites another to change but does not demand it."
3. This way of seeing the connection between God, ourselves, and others was first described to me by Ron Claassen, the founder of Victim Offender Reconciliation Program in Fresno, California.
4. One difficulty with discussing nonresistance is that it is advocated by several unrelated groups. When I speak of Anabaptists I refer to those sixteenth-century persons who created the free church during Reformation times. When Anabaptist is used as an adjective, it refers to something consistent with the thought of Anabaptists, particularly the thought of the Swiss Brethren who originated in Ulrich Zwingli's circle in Zurich, then broke away from him when he tried to keep the tie between church and state.
  More will be said about the rise and development of Anabaptism, and of the particular stream of Anabaptism we will be following. "Mennonite" is often used in this work as a generic term for the spiritual descendants of the Anabaptists,

with apologies to other historic peace churches who claim that same heritage, but not the same name.

Chapter 2

1. Scott Reeves, "120 Arrested at Abortion Clinic Protest," *The Fresno Bee*, 12 March 1989, A1.

2. For a fuller discussion of the judicial system of the United States and Canada as it relates to violence, see Duane Ruth-Heffelbower, *The Christia.. and Jury Duty* (Akron, Pa.: Mennonite Central Committee, 1987). A revision has also been published by Herald Press, 1991.

3. The adversary system is the method of having two or more sides each putting on their cases as best they can, trying to convince the judge or jury that they are right, and the other side is wrong.

4. A classic work in this area is Frederick Perls, Ralph Hefferline, and Paul Goodman, *Gestalt Therapy* (New York: Bantam Books, 1980).

5. A very accessible discussion of how anger influences relationships can be found in David Augsburger, *Caring Enough to Confront* (Scottdale, Pa.: Herald Press, 1973).

Chapter 3

1. I am aware of writers who question this long-established comparison between Greek and Hebrew viewpoints but have not found their explanations fully convincing. The reader should be aware of the scholarly disagreement in this area of study.

2. Perry Yoder has produced an excellent exposition of the word *shalom* in *Shalom: The Bible's Word for Salvation, Justice, and Peace* (Newton, Kan.: Faith and Life Press, 1987).

3. Vernard Eller has treated this same line of reasoning in a readable way in *Christian Anarchy* (Grand Rapids, Mich.: William B. Eerdmans Publishing Company, 1987). Eller demonstrates this same explanation of civil religion, but then, based upon a faulty premise, argues in favor of it! My review of Eller's book, including an explanation of this faulty premise, can be found in *The Christian Century*, 2 March 1988, p. 220.

4. The choices available to Marilyn Miller in her translation of this important passage are detailed in Barclay M. Newman and Eugene A. Nida, *A Translator's Handbook on Paul's Letter to the Romans* (Stuttgart, Germany: United Bible Societies, 1973), pp. 165-6.

5. The Rocky Flats plant was closed due to massive radioactive contamination in 1989. Many pounds of highly toxic plutonium were discovered in the air ducts of the plant, besides much other contamination in the surrounding area.

6. For an extended discussion of this phenomenon see Jacques Ellul, *The Subversion of Christianity*, trans. Geoffrey W. Bromiley (Grand Rapids, Mich.: William B. Eerdmans Publishing Company, 1986).

Chapter 4

1. For an excellent and popularly written description of the impact of the Turks on Europe, see Merle Severy, "The World of Suleiman the Magnificent," *National Geographic*, November 1987, pp. 552-601.

2. The process by which Anabaptists came to a semblance of unity on these principles is detailed in James M. Stayer, *Anabaptism and the Sword* (Lawrence, Kan.: Coronado Press, 1976). I have adopted his analysis in this chapter.

3. Guy F. Hershberger, *War, Peace, and Nonresistance* (Scottdale, Pa.: Herald Press, 1944, revised 1969).
4. Albert N. Keim and Grant M. Stoltzfus, *The Politics of Conscience* (Scottdale, Pa.: Herald Press, 1988).

Chapter 5
1. Adapted from a lecture by Cornelius J. Dyck, March 10, 1988, at Associated Mennonite Biblical Seminaries, Elkhart, Ind., based on Walter Klaassen, ed., *Anabaptism in Outline* (Scottdale, Pa.: Herald Press, 1981), pp. 41-42.
2. C. J. Dyck, "The Anabaptist Understanding of the Good News," in *Anabaptism and Mission*, ed. Wilbert R. Shenk (Scottdale, Pa.: Herald Press, 1984), p. 29.
3. C. J. Dyck, unpublished lecture notes based upon material previously published under the title "Sinners and Saints."
4. William E. Keeney, *The Development of Dutch Anabaptist Thought and Practice from 1539-1564* (Nieuwkoop, Netherlands: B. DeGraaf, 1968), pp. 67-9; "Original Sin," *The Mennonite Encyclopedia*, vol. 4 (Scottdale, Pa.: Herald Press, 1959) pp. 79-83.
5. Ibid., p. 71.
6. William Klassen, "The Role of the Child in Anabaptism," in *Mennonite Images*, ed. Harry Loewen (Winnipeg, Man.: Hyperion Press Limited, 1980), p. 19.
7. Ibid.
8. Robert Friedmann, *The Theology of Anabaptism* (Scottdale, Pa.: Herald Press, 1973), p. 27.
9. *The Complete Writings of Menno Simons* (CWMS), trans. Leonard Verduin, ed. J.C. Wenger, "Confession of the Distressed Christians" (Scottdale, Pa.: Herald Press, 1984), p. 506.
10. Friedmann, pp. 58-60.
11. Dyck, "Good News," in *Anabaptism and Mission*, p. 29.
12. Friedmann, pp. 71-72.
13. CWMS, "The New Birth," p. 91.
14. CWMS, "The New Birth," p. 93.
15. George H. Williams, ed., *Spiritual and Anabaptist Writers*, The Library of Christian Classics (Philadelphia, Pa.: The Westminster Press, 1957), p. 80.
16. Leland Harder, ed., *The Sources of Swiss Anabaptism* (Scottdale, Pa.: Herald Press, 1985), p. 284.
17. Ray S. Anderson, *On Being Human: Essays in Theological Anthropology* (Grand Rapids, Mich.: William B. Eerdmans Publishing Company, 1982), p. 171.
18. *The Christian Leader* (Hillsboro, Kans.), 8 November 1988, p. 23.
19. Guy F. Hershberger, *War, Peace, and Nonresistance* (Scottdale, Pa.: Herald Press, 1944) p. 216.
20. Reinhold Niebuhr, *Moral Man and Immoral Society* (New York: Charles Scribner's Sons, 1932), p. 264.

Chapter 6
1. Albert N. Keim and Grant M. Stoltzfus, *The Politics of Conscience* (Scottdale, Pa.: Herald Press, 1988), p. 26.
2. Quoted in Urbane Peachey, ed., *Mennonite Statements on Peace and Social Concerns, 1900-1978* (Akron, Pa.: Mennonite Central Committee, 1980), p. 130.
3. This story from Jep Hostetler, collected by Phil Stoltzfus for Christian Peacemaker Teams, is based upon an interview in the *Mennonite Distorter*, vol. 2,

no. 5, February 1988. Jep teaches in the Department of Preventive Medicine at Ohio State University.

4. The fear of lost tax exemption was a large issue in the discussions of delegates to General Conference Mennonite Church Triennial sessions in 1977, 1980, and 1983 when withholding of employee taxes was discussed. A variety of methods were discussed to allow the conference to cease its tax collection activities without risking the loss of tax exempt status.

5. Recorded March 1988 for Christian Peacemaker Teams by Phil Stoltzfus. This story has been published in *MCC Peace Office Newsletter*, vol. 19, no. 2.

Chapter 7
1. All of the quotations which follow are from news stories in *The Fresno Bee* on the dates listed.

2. Scott Reeves, "120 Arrested at Abortion Clinic Protest," *The Fresno Bee*, 12 March 1989.

3. Charles McCarthy, "No Gag Order in Abortion Trial," *The Fresno Bee*, 22 September 1989.

4. Charles McCarthy, "Lawyer Faces Jail When Trial Ends," *The Fresno Bee*, 3 November 1989.

5. Alex Pulaski, "Hung Jury in Fresno Abortion Trial," *The Fresno Bee*, 9 November 1989.

6. Charles McCarthy, "Demonstrators Given Conditional Sentences," *The Fresno Bee*, 3 March 1990.

7. Charles Scriven, "The Reformation Radicals Ride Again," *Christianity Today*, 5 March 1990, p. 13.

8. Ibid., p. 15.

9. This story first appeared in Peace Section Newsletter, vol. XV, no. 3, May-June 1985).

10. Stanley Hauerwas and William Willimon, "Peculiar People," *Christianity Today*, 5 March 1990, p. 18.

11. Ronald J. Sider, *Nonviolence: The Invincible Weapon?* (Dallas: Word Publishing, 1989), p. 81.

Bibliography

Anderson, Ray S. *On Being Human: Essays in Theological Anthropology*. Grand Rapids, Mich.: William B. Eerdmans Publishing Company, 1982.

Augsburger, David. *Caring Enough to Confront*. Scottdale, Pa.: Herald Press, 1973.

Barrett, Lois. *The Way God Fights*. Scottdale, Pa.: Herald Press, 1987.

Dyck, Cornelius J., ed. *An Introduction to Mennonite History*. Scottdale, Pa.: Herald Press, 1967.

_____. "The Anabaptist Understanding of the Good News," in *Anabaptism and Mission*, ed. Wilbert R. Shenk. Scottdale, Pa.: Herald Press, 1984.

Eller, Vernard. *Christian Anarchy*. Grand Rapids, Mich.: William B. Eerdmans Publishing Company, 1987.

Ellul, Jacques. *The Subversion of Christianity*. Grand Rapids, Mich.: William B. Eerdmans Publishing Company, 1986.

Estep, William R. *The Anabaptist Story*. Grand Rapids, Mich.: William B. Eerdmans Publishing Co., 1973.

Friedmann, Robert. *The Theology of Anabaptism*. Scottdale, Pa.: Herald Press, 1973.

Friesen, Duane K. *Christian Peacemaking and International Conflict*. Scottdale, Pa.: Herald Press, 1986.

Harder, Leland ed., *The Sources of Swiss Anabaptism*. Scottdale, Pa.: Herald Press, 1985.

Hauerwas, Stanley, and William Willimon, "Peculiar People," *Christianity Today*, 5 March 1990, 18.

Heffelbower, Duane. "The Christian and Civil Disobedience," *Direction*, vol. 15, no. 1, (Spring, 1986), pp. 23-30.

Hershberger, Guy F. *War, Peace, and Nonresistance*. Scottdale, Pa.: Herald Press, 1944.

Keeney, William E. *The Development of Dutch Anabaptist Thought and Practice from 1539-1564*. Nieuwkoop, Netherlands: B. DeGraaf, 1968.

Keim, Albert N., and Grant M. Stoltzfus. *The Politics of Conscience*. Scottdale, Pa.: Herald Press, 1988.

Klaassen, Walter, ed. *Anabaptism in Outline*. Scottdale, Pa.: Herald Press, 1981.

_____. *Anabaptism: Neither Catholic nor Protestant*. Waterloo, Ont.: Conrad Press, 1973.

Klassen, William. *Covenant and Community. The Life, Writings and Hermeneutics of Pilgrim Marpeck*. Grand Rapids, Mich.: William B. Eerdmans Publishing Company, 1968.

_____. *Love of Enemies: The Way to Peace*. Philadelphia, Pa.: Fortress Press, 1984.

_____. "The Role of the Child in Anabaptism," in *Mennonite Images*, ed. Harry Loewen. Winnipeg, Man.: Hyperion Press Limited, 1980.

Niebuhr, Reinhold. *Moral Man and Immoral Society*. New York: Charles Scribner's Sons, 1932.

Perls, Frederick, Ralph Hefferline, and Paul Goodman. *Gestalt Therapy*. New York: Bantam Books, 1980.

Ruth-Heffelbower, Duane. *The Christian and Jury Duty*. Akron, Pa.: Mennonite Central Committee, 1987.

Charles Scriven, "The Reformation Radicals Ride Again," *Christianity Today*, 5 March 1990, 13.

Sider, Ronald J. *Nonviolence: The Invincible Weapon?* Dallas: Word Publishing, 1989.

Stayer, James M. *Anabaptism and the Sword*. Lawrence, Kans.: Coronado Press, 1976.

Wenger, J. C. *Pacifism and Biblical Nonresistance*. Focal Pamphlet No. 15. Scottdale, Pa.: Herald Press, 1968.

Williams, George H. ed., *Spiritual and Anabaptist Writers*, The Library of Christian Classics. Philadelphia, Pa.: The Westminster Press, 1957.

Yoder, John Howard. *The Politics of Jesus*. Grand Rapids, Mich.: William B. Eerdmans Publishing Company, 1972.

The Author

After eleven years of law practice, Duane Ruth-Heffelbower
closed his law office to enter seminary. He is, with his wife, Clare
Ann Ruth-Heffelbower, a founding copastor of Peace Community
Church—Mennonite, of Clovis,
California, where he and Clare
Ann continue to serve.

For a number of years Duane
has worked professionally as a
mediator. He continues to provide mediation and coun-
seling services. He was involved in the creation of the
Fresno, California, Victim Offender Reconciliation Program and works with the program as an active peacemaker.

Duane is also a volunteer chaplain for the local police
department. Having served as coordinator of Develop-

mental Disabilities Services for West Coast Mennonite Central Committee, he continues to be involved with developmental disabilities issues.

Duane has had both legal and theological training and experience, with a B.A. from Kansas State University, a doctor of jurisprudence (J.D.) degree from Golden Gate University, San Francisco,(Calif.), and an M.Div. from Mennonite Biblical Seminary, Elkhart, Indiana. He was a captain in the United States Air Force. This background, combined with his involvement in justice issues through law practice and his participation in community-based justice programs both as lawyer and pastor, helps him bring a unique perspective to the question of how we make peace in a dangerous world.

Growing up in Newton, Kansas, Duane was heavily involved in church life. After marrying Clare Ann, he became involved in General Conference Mennonite Church work, serving on the General Board, Division of Administration, and Spiritual Emphasis Committee. Duane and Clare Ann currently serve on a part-time basis as Evangelism and Church Development staff for Pacific District Conference (G.C.). Duane and Clare Ann have a son, Andrew.